BEATRIX POTTER™
FIGURES & GIFTWARE

Design by Bill King, King Design & Print, Ipswich, Suffolk

Photography by Mark Ward, Elm Studios, Ipswich, Suffolk

Phototypesetting by Brian Rogers, Ipswich, Suffolk

Film origination by Claydongraphic, Claydon, Ipswich, Suffolk

Printing and binding by Alderman Printing & Bookbinding Co Ltd, Ipswich, Suffolk

Published and distributed by UK International Ceramics Ltd, 10 Wilford Bridge Spur, Melton, Woodbridge, Suffolk IP12 1RJ, England.

ISBN 0 9517772 6 2

FIRST PUBLISHED 1992
SECOND EDITION 1996

Beatrix Potter is a Registered Trade Mark of Frederick Warne & Co.

John Beswick & Royal Albert

BEATRIX POTTER™
FIGURES & GIFTWARE

Louise Irvine, Valerie Baynton, Harry Sales,
Graham Tongue, Sal Castillo, Nick Tzimas

Studio of Royal Doulton
England

ROYAL ALBERT
ENGLAND

PUBLISHED BY
UK International Ceramics
10 Wilford Bridge Spur, Melton, Woodbridge, Suffolk, IP12 1RJ, England

Editor's Acknowledgements and Introduction to the Second Edition

We were delighted with the reception for the first edition of this book and have appreciated all the comments and information sent to us by collectors and dealers around the world. New backstamps and colour variations have come to light and these have been included in the relevant sections of this second edition. We have also incorporated all the new introductions and discontinuations since 1992 and started a new section for the collection of large size figures launched in 1993.

The growing interest in Beatrix Potter series ware has prompted the inclusion of a new chapter and there is now a reference list of Beatrix Potter books with the figures they inspired. We hope these new sections will add to collectors' enjoyment of the book.

I should like to thank everybody who has assisted in the production of both editions of this book, especially Gordon Hopper who loaned his entire collection for photography. Help in locating some of the rarer model and colour variations was also given by Harvey May, Tom Hood, Bob and Irene Davidge, Martin and Josie Hogg and Grahame Davis. Several keen collectors have provided useful information, in particular Nina Mullins and John Canter. Maureen Batkin and Richard Dennis have provided helpful details about the early Beatrix Potter tableware.

I am also indebted to Graham Tongue, Harry Sales and Peter Roberts for explaining their roles in the production of the World of Beatrix Potter collection and to Richard Halliday and Tracey Richards at Royal Doulton for information on new introductions. My thanks also to Emma Collins and Barbara Groome for typing the original listings, and to Zoë Gilligan for her work on the second edition.

Finally, I should like to thank Nick Tzimas for making this book possible, my husband George for his constant encouragement and my son Ben for giving me a good excuse to rediscover the wonderful tales of Beatrix Potter.

Louise Irvine

Publisher's Acknowledgements

We would like to thank Mrs Mary Moorcroft, Public Relations Executive at Royal Doulton, Ms Nicola Lello, Ms Claire Morris and Mr Kevin Bennett, for supplying photographs and information about Beatrix Potter products.

We are especially grateful to Ms Valerie Baynton, Mr Harry Sales, Mr Graham Tongue and Mr Sal Castillo for supplying various chapters for the book. Special thanks also to Mrs Deborah Bates, Assistant Company Secretary of Royal Doulton, for her co-operation in the production of this book.

Finally our special thanks to Ms Louise Irvine and Mr Paul Tzimas whose ideas and enthusiasm largely inspired this book.

Nick Tzimas

4

CONTENTS

Photo by courtesy of Victoria & Albert Museum.

Beatrix Potter, aged 23

THE STORY OF BEATRIX POTTER

LOUISE IRVINE

IN 1893 Beatrix Potter wrote a picture letter about the adventures of a rabbit called Peter to amuse a sick young child and now, a century later, he is one of the world's best loved nursery characters. *The Tale of Peter Rabbit* was privately printed in book form when Beatrix failed to find a publisher and it was distributed to all her friends and relations in time for Christmas 1901. Meanwhile the search for a commercial publisher continued and an agreement was reached with Frederick Warne and Company to produce a coloured edition in 1902. The little book was an immediate success and it has remained continuously in print ever since in many different languages.

Peter Rabbit was followed by a succession of tales about animal characters, such as Squirrel Nutkin, Benjamin Bunny, Mrs Tittlemouse and Jemima Puddle-Duck, all of whom have delighted young and old alike. Their personalities evolved from Beatrix's studies of her own pets and the animals she observed during her family's long summer holidays in Scotland and the Lake District. Her childhood sketchbooks are filled with meticulous studies from nature as well as fantasies about rabbits engaged in human pursuits and this obvious skill in drawing was encouraged from an early age. Back home in London, animals were smuggled into the schoolroom to serve as models and these pets became increasingly important to her as she was denied contact with friends her own age, leading a solitary existence with all the restrictions of a conventional middle-class Victorian household. Over the years her menagerie included a frog called Punch, two lizards named Toby and Judy, a cock robin, a bat, guinea pigs, a dormouse with the curious name of Xarifa and several rabbits, in particular Benjamin Bouncer. He was the model for her first commercial drawings, a series of six designs for cards, which she sold in 1890 at the age of 24.

Benjamin was succeeded by another rabbit, which she named Peter Piper, and she became equally devoted to him, spending hours sketching him from every conceivable angle. He was also the model for several card designs as well as the inspiration for the picture letter which launched her publishing career. Gradually more animals joined her entourage and became the subjects of later tales, notably Tom Thumb and Hunca Munca, who starred in *The Tale of Two Bad Mice* (1904) and her hedgehog, Mrs Tiggy-Winkle, whose adventures as a washer-woman were published in 1905.

This was a particularly creative period for Beatrix for, not only was she illustrating two books a year, she had also produced a Peter Rabbit doll, a board game and some wallpaper designs. These 'side-shows', as she described her character merchandise, feature regularly in her correspondence with Norman Warne who looked after all her business interests on behalf of her publishers. They became close friends and in 1905 Norman proposed marriage. Beatrix accepted, despite her

© F. Warne & Co., 1955
Pen and ink drawing of
'The Rabbit's Dream'

parents' objections to the match, but tragically Norman died within the year and she sought solace in her work, producing three new titles for 1906, *The Tale of Mr Jeremy Fisher, The Story of a Fierce Bad Rabbit* and *The Story of Miss Moppet.* She began to spend all her spare time in the

© F. Warne & Co., 1902, 1987
Illustration from
'The Tale of Peter Rabbit'

Lake District where she had bought some property from the profits of her books and an aunt's legacy. Hill Top at Sawrey, a working farm, became her private sanctuary and it is now visited by Beatrix Potter fans from all over the world who delight in identifying the interiors and surrounding landscapes used in *The Tale of Tom Kitten* (1907), *The Tale of Jemima Puddle-Duck* (1908), *The Roly Poly Pudding* (1908) and others.

Around this period Beatrix was modelling some little clay figures of her characters which she described as 'life-like and comical' and she was in correspondence with the Royal Doulton pottery in Lambeth about reproducing them. She had been referred to Joseph Mott, the Art Director, by her friend Katherine Smallfield, who was a decorator at the Lambeth studio, and a surviving letter of January 1908 indicates that she planned to visit the pottery when

National Trust Photographic Library/Richard Surman.

Front of Hill Top Cottage, home of Beatrix Potter.

the weather improved. It is not known whether a meeting ever took place, although Beatrix recalled in a later letter to her publishers that Mr Mott was 'very keen on making figures of my animals'. However, the matter was complicated by a prior agreement with a German firm which authorised them to make a range of nursery ware. Beatrix was not pleased with the results, complaining that they had 'turned out something so ugly in the way of a tea set' and urged her publishers to get rid of them or at least alter the contract so that she could offer the statuettes to other firms.

No more was mentioned about these clay figures until 1917 when Beatrix received a model of Jemima Puddle-Duck which had been produced by the daughter of Leonard Grimwade, a pottery manufacturer in Stoke-on-Trent.

National Trust Photographic Library/Peter Baistow.

Interior of Hill Top showing some of Beatrix Potter's china collection

Beatrix's reaction was unfavourable and she wrote to her publisher 'It is a very embarrassing bird. It is not bad, but compared with my own models it is rather commonplace'. Presumably this incident prompted her to start modelling again for a few months later she announced that she had made 'rather a good clay Peter' and acquired a modelling spoon.

A selection of her models was sent to the Grimwade pottery but most of them were broken in transit. However, Elsie Grimwade was able to see the style and scale that was required and set about modelling another Jemima Puddle-Duck which could be easily moulded. According to the surviving correspondence, Beatrix liked the second model, although not the colouring, and in response Miss Grimwade suggested that perhaps her father could come to some arrangement with Royal Doulton as they had better facilities for colouring figures at their Burslem pottery. Beatrix favoured this idea as she thought that Doulton's had 'some well modelled and glazed animals selling now' but it would appear nothing came of the suggestion. Elsie Grimwade is known to have modelled Jeremy Fisher and Tom Kitten but she did not continue with the project as she was required to nurse her mother and so the second attempt to reproduce Beatrix Potter's characters in clay was thwarted. Grimwade's did, however, produce a range of nursery ware with litho printed decoration of Peter Rabbit and friends. Although Beatrix gave her permission in 1917, in an attempt to curb the pirated china on the market, Grimwade's did not actually begin manufacturing until 1922, blaming war-time shortages of materials and staff. Beatrix was irritated by the long delay and at one time considered finding another company but she was very pleased with the final results and ordered a selection for Christmas presents.

The pattern of Beatrix's life had changed dramatically by the 1920s and most of her time was spent looking after the farms she had acquired in the Lake District where she now lived with her husband

Royal Albert nursery ware

William Heelis. He was the local solicitor who handled all her property and she came to rely on his kindness and support. They were married in 1913 and thereafter Beatrix found it increasingly difficult to find the time or the inclination to write new books. She was, however, keen to support Warne and Company who had experienced some financial difficulties during the war and so, in the post war years, she revived some early ideas and sketches in order to produce two painting books, two collections of nursery rhymes, a story based on one of Aesop's fables *The Tale*

Duchess in the porch from
'The Pie and the Patty Pan'

of Johnny Town-Mouse (1918) and an almanac for 1929. By this time she complained that her eyesight was failing but she was still motivated to produce a series of fund-raising watercolours to save a stretch of Lake Windermere foreshore from development. During this period of renewed activity she also wrote *The Fairy Caravan* (1929) for an American publisher and *The Tale of Little Pig Robinson* (1930) and the royalties from these two books were used to assist the National Trust acquire some land at Coniston. In all, Beatrix left over 4,000 acres in Cumbria to the Trust, thus ensuring the preservation of the countryside she loved so much.

According to Beatrix she was finally 'written out' but, although by now in her late sixties, she showed no signs of slowing down with her other interests, in particular the breeding of Herdwick sheep. Her name had become well known in many parts of the world and there was a steady stream of correspondence from fans, especially Americans, some of whom made the journey to Sawrey to meet her. Although she did not encourage personal publicity, critical essays about her work occasionally appeared in the press and one of these inspired her to dig out an unfinished story

*Presentation box for the
John Beswick plaques*

and complete it. *Wag by Wall* was due to be published in America in 1944 but Beatrix did not see the finished book as she died on December 22, 1943. The following month the New York Herald Tribune described her many qualities and summarised 'Beatrix Potter, North-country farmer, connoisseur of old furniture and *china*, lover of nature and animals, was an artist both with words and brush'. (Author's italics).

Beatrix Potter's enthusiasm for pottery and china is clearly illustrated in the collection she built up at Hill Top, as well as in her response to Grimwade's nursery ware, and she would surely have been gratified by all the interest shown in her work by ceramic manufacturers after her death. In 1947 John Beswick of Longton was given the rights to reproduce her characters as small scale earthenware figures, at last fulfilling one of Beatrix Potter's early ambitions. Two years later Wedgwood were licensed to produce Peter Rabbit nursery ware and more recently Royal Albert have been authorised to make tableware and gift ware featuring some of the other characters from Beatrix Potter's books. Royal Albert and John Beswick are now both part of the Royal Doulton group and since 1989 the Royal Albert backstamp has been used on the figure models as well as the nursery ware. In the light of Beatrix Potter's early interest in the Royal Doulton potteries, it is a curious coincidence that this company is now responsible for producing such a wide range of Beatrix Potter wares.

Selection of Grimwade's nursery ware

BEATRIX POTTER FIGURES

VALERIE BAYNTON

THE idea to introduce a Beatrix Potter figure collection originated during a holiday in the Lake District taken by Ewart Beswick, the Chairman and Managing Director of the company, and his Cumbrian-born wife, Lucy. After visiting the haunts of Beatrix Potter, Mrs Beswick returned to Stoke-on-Trent and made a point of visiting the company's chief modeller, Arthur Gredington, in his studio. During their conversation she suggested that Jemima Puddle-Duck would look rather nice as a figure and without further ado Arthur began to produce a clay model. He took as the basis of his design her portrait in *The Tale of Jemima Puddle-Duck* where she appears dressed in a blue poke bonnet and purple shawl, setting out to look for a secret nesting place. In June 1947 Jemima was ready to be inspected by Ewart Beswick. He and the other directors gave their approval and so copyright permission was obtained from the publishers of the tales, Frederick Warne and Company, for the production and sale of ceramic Beatrix Potter figures.

Arthur Gredington was directed to model further characters from the tales and the decoration of each study was the responsibility of the Art Director, James Hayward. As each model had to reproduce faithfully the colours and details found in the original book illustrations, individual decorations were not recorded in the master pattern book. Instead one decoration number was issued, 8894, with the annotation — 'Beatrix

Advertisement for the introductory collection of Beatrix Potter figures c 1950

ABOVE RIGHT: Mouldmaker Albert Hallam at work on a plaster case, from which the working moulds are made

RIGHT: Here the figures are being taken out of the moulds by the maker, Mrs. Slinn. The figures are made by the process of casting with clay slip

ABOVE: After underglaze painting and glazing the figures are here seen being placed on a truck by Richard Derricott prior to being fired in the glost kiln

BELOW: Painting underglaze and onglaze. Misses Mary Axon, Irene Fernyhough, Marjorie Bradshaw and Marjorie Thorley

Illustrations for an article in 'Pottery & Glass' magazine, June 1950

Potter's Animal Characters in original colours executed in under-glaze and enamel colours'.

Once the colours had been approved by the publishers, James Hayward would paint a figure which would then be used as the standard and copied by the Beswick painter responsible for the decoration of each piece.

The most popular subjects were selected to form the first collection, which was launched in 1948, and *Jemima Puddle-Duck* was joined by *Peter Rabbit, Tom Kitten, Timmy Tiptoes, Squirrel Nutkin, Mrs Tittlemouse, Little Pig Robinson, Benjamin Bunny, Samuel Whiskers* and *Mrs Tiggy-Winkle*. Initially the figures could not be sold in Great Britain because war-time restrictions were still in force and so they were launched in America, Canada, Australia,

Arthur Gredington

New Zealand, Rhodesia and Sweden. The first customer feedback thus came from overseas and an American collector wrote to the company: 'They are perfect because they are exactly like the original illustrations, no one has tried to improve on them or add their own ideas. To my mind that exactly describes these works of art that you have produced with such fidelity for Beatrix Potter admirers who are legion'.

The *Publishers Circular and Booksellers Record* of 1950 also praised them, commenting that: 'The colourings are full, the figures most natural and the whole present beautiful *objects d'art'*.

The Beatrix Potter collection grew steadily during the 1950s and 60s with Mr. Gredington contributing sixteen more characters, most of which are still in production today. The first withdrawal in 1967 was the now very rare model of *Duchess*, the Pomeranian dog, carrying a bunch of flowers which was modelled by Graham Orwell. Many of the modellers who have worked in the Beswick studios since 1947 have been involved with creating the figures and details are given later in the book.

Inspiration for new designs came from the tales themselves. James Hayward recalled that the entire collection of Beatrix Potter books belonging to Ewart and Lucy's daughter, Judith,

Beatrix Potter Collector's Plates

The first and second of a series of Beatrix Potter Collector's plates are now available portraying characters from her famous children's story books.

Jemima Puddleduck and Foxy Whiskered Gentleman are featured on the first plate and on the second, we see Peter Rabbit in typically mischievous mood in a vegetable patch.

Supplied individually, the plates come in a delightfully illustrated presentation box.

Catalogue illustration of collectors plaques: Jemima Puddle-Duck and Foxy Whiskered Gentleman and Peter Rabbit

The first five Studio Sculptures: Peter Rabbit, Mr Jeremy Fisher, Mrs Tiggy-Winkle,
Timmy Willie and Flopsy Bunnies

found their way into the modelling studio where their pages were (and still are) turned as the artists searched for new subjects. Every model is created with immense care to ensure that each is an exact representation of the character as originally drawn by Beatrix Potter, right down to the last button on *Samuel Whisker's* waistcoat or the inquisitive expression on *Peter Rabbit's* face. However, the modeller does have some creative freedom because frequently only one view of a character is portrayed in the tales and, as the figures are three dimensional, the back and sides have to be imagined. Every design has to be approved by Copyrights, the licensing agents working on behalf of Frederick Warne, and the total creative process can take six months.

Mrs Lucy Beswick remained involved with the development of the collection and would see each figure as it was modelled and painted. She also visited the under-glaze and on-glaze departments, where the characters were painted, to ensure that the correct decorations were followed. This concern with quality and accuracy continues to be important today and stringent quality control is carried out at all stages of production.

The figures are portrayed in a variety of ways, some in the setting as they appear in the tales, for example *The Old Woman Who Lived In A Shoe* is shown in her shoe house surrounded by some of her children, *The Tailor of Gloucester* is studying *The Tailor and Cutter* and

Mrs Tiggy-Winkle has an iron in her hand, poised to begin pressing the next shirt. Other models, especially many of the earlier introductions, are portrait studies which capture the character in typical pose, for example *Tom Kitten* and *Mr Benjamin Bunny*. Under the direction of Design Manager, Graham Tongue, the models became more complicated and adventurous in format. Few characters are shown in static pose nowadays. They are more likely to carry out an action as with *Mr Jeremy Fisher Digging* and *Little Pig Robinson Spying*.

By 1964 characters from 21 of the 23 Beatrix Potter classic tales had been selected for production but it was not until 1977 that all the tales had been used, following the introduction of *Fierce Bad Rabbit* from the book of the same name and *Pickles* from the *Tale of Ginger and Pickles*. Even today some of her tales are more popular than others. *The Tale of Benjamin Bunny* and *Appley Dapply's Nursery Rhymes* have contributed the most characters whilst *The Tale of Miss Moppet* and *The Story of Fierce Bad Rabbit* have been the least influential with only one character from each appearing in the collection.

The figures have been successful ever since their launch and consequently other collectable items and accessories have been introduced over the years. The lamp base in the form of a tree was a popular display item for over

Royal Albert tea ware

twenty years and this was sold either on its own or with a choice of figure. Since 1970 collectors have also been able to buy a display stand, modelled to resemble gnarled and knotted wood, with space for six Beatrix Potter figures.

In 1967, three favourite characters were modelled in the form of wall plaques but these only remained in production until 1969. The idea was repeated in 1977 with three new subjects modelled in low relief on square plaques but again they met with limited success. Perhaps the most novel additions to the collection have been the six character jugs introduced in 1987 and 1988. The subjects chosen — *Old Mr Brown, Jeremy Fisher, Peter Rabbit, Jemima Puddle-Duck, Mrs Tiggy-Winkle* and *Tom Kitten* — are particularly suited to the humorous modelling synonymous with character jugs.

During the 1980s the Beswick factory experimented with a bonded ceramic body and five Beatrix Potter characters were introduced in 1984 as part of a collection of *Studio Sculptures*. The first five models — *Timmy Willie, Mr Jeremy Fisher, Mrs Tiggy-Winkle, Peter Rabbit* and *Flopsy Bunnies* — were joined in 1985 by two more — *Yock-Yock* and *Peter Rabbit in the Watering Can*. They were all the result of many hours of

Peter Rabbit, Jeremy Fisher and Old Mr Brown character jugs

Jemima Puddle-Duck, Tom Kitten and Mrs Tiggy-Winkle character jugs

detailed modelling and were carefully painted by hand in the John Beswick studios but they only remained in production until the end of 1983. Because of their different appearance, collectors do not usually classify them along with the other Beatrix Potter figures and they are not easy to find today. The delightful study of Timmy Willie curled up in a pea pod was later remodelled and joined the standard Beatrix Potter collection as *Timmy Willie Sleeping*.

In 1987 a range of tableware and gift ware featuring Beatrix Potter's characters was launched with the Royal Albert backstamp. The designs were drawn in the Royal Albert studio, under the direction of Peter Roberts, and they are all taken from Miss Potter's original illustrations. The diverse collection includes story sets, nursery ware, florals, decorative wall plates, money balls and special christening gifts and new items are added each year.

The tableware and figures collections were combined under the famous Royal Albert name in 1989. All the Beswick traditions have been preserved and the models continue to be created, produced and painted with the same attention to detail.

To date there has been a choice of 96 standard size characters and 42 of these have been discontinued. There is also a new collection of large size figures, which began with Peter Rabbit in 1993 and now totals 8 favourite characters with more to come. Collectors can select a theme, such as characters from a specific tale, or all those from the stories written at Hill Top (the home of Beatrix Potter) or they can choose a breed such as mice, rabbits or cats. Unusual wildlife not often discovered in ceramic, such as insects and moles, can also be found and would make an interesting and colourful addition to a collection.

For the more ambitious it is not impossible to find all the models introduced since 1947 and there will undoubtedly be many more in the future. Each new introduction reflects the fascinating history of the people involved in the creative process. It is a unique collection which combines a timeless quality and artistry with the legend and appeal of Beatrix Potter.

Mrs Tittlemouse plaque.

DESIGNING BEATRIX POTTER FIGURES

HARRY SALES

I JOINED the Beswick factory in 1960 as assistant to the Art Director, James Hayward, and the plan was for me to take over his job when he retired. I was therefore involved in all the creative developments of the factory from that time, including the Beatrix Potter range which was already

Harry Sales

well established and highly successful. It was my responsibility to select new characters from the books and produce working drawings for the modellers, choosing poses that would be suitable for the pottery medium. At the beginning I worked with Albert Hallam, the head modeller, but gradually I ensured that all new modelling staff were familiar with the Beatrix Potter series in order to maintain continuity of this important product through the years.

The licensees, Frederick Warne and Company, were particularly strict, both in regard to the shape and the decoration of the figures, and great care had to be taken to achieve their high standards of reproduction. I frequently travelled to London to discuss the prototypes and confirm final approval to manufacture and, although this was very time consuming, the resulting

Albert Hallam

quality was the basis of the continued success of the series.

Extending the series over the years became increasingly difficult due to the finite number of characters in the Beatrix Potter books and I overcame this by introducing existing subjects in different poses as well as double character models. Also, in an attempt to extend the collection in different directions, I designed some wall plaques which I modelled along with David Lyttleton.

It was also my responsibility to deal with customer enquiries and through contact with so many ardent collectors throughout the world, I learned much about the reasons for the huge success of the Beatrix Potter characters. It was generally believed at the time that the figures were bought just for children but it soon became clear to me that this was also a serious collectable area for adults. Their attention to colour, detail and faithful reproduction was incredible and even the slightest variation attracted comment. As different editions of the little books often had variations in colour, our correspondence sometimes became complicated!

I look back on my involvement with the Beatrix Potter range with great affection and am proud to have been instrumental in maintaining the true qualities of this remarkable lady's work. It was truly for me a labour of love.

*Design for the figure of Tabitha Twitchit and
Miss Moppet by Harry Sales*

PRODUCING BEATRIX POTTER FIGURES

GRAHAM TONGUE

IT was in 1966 when I joined the Beswick Studio that I first heard the term 'BP'. When I asked what this meant I was told 'Beatrix Potter, of course!'. I started by modelling a few figures but it was not until 1986, when I became Design Manager, that I really began to be involved with the whole process. Since then I have been a frequent visitor to Hill Top — the home of Beatrix Potter — where I admit I love to go because I really get the feeling of the stories taking place.

Graham Tongue and Martyn Alcock discussing the original clay model for Peter and the Red Pocket Handkerchief

We try to introduce at least three new models each year, but this gets increasingly more difficult as the most popular characters were all modelled in the early years. The first step in introducing a new model is the preparation of a sketch which is then approved for marketing. It is then given to one of the modellers who will take about two weeks to create a three dimensional clay model. On completion of the original clay model, a plaster of Paris master mould is made from it and sometimes, to simplify the shape for production, a head or arm may have to be removed and moulded separately. This process takes just over a week.

When the mould is dry it goes to the casting department where liquid clay is poured in to make the first cast. After about thirty minutes the figure is ready to be removed and it is taken to a sponger who will carefully rub off the seams. It is then allowed to dry out slowly before it goes on to the first firing stage which takes approximately thirteen and a half hours at a temperature of 1200°C. The firing turns the delicate clay into a hard 'biscuit' body which can now go on to the first stage of decoration.

A painter will now accurately copy the colours from the illustrations in Beatrix Potter's books. This stage is called under-glaze painting and when

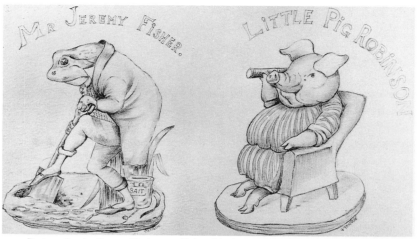

Designs for the figures Mr Jeremy Fisher Digging and Little Pig Robinson Spying by Graham Tongue

complete the figure is ready for the second firing which hardens the colour. This process takes approximately ten hours at a temperature of 774°C. The figure is now ready for its glazed surface and this is done by a dipper who will submerge the model in a suspension of ground glaze and water. After this has dried, the figure is then fired for the third time for approximately fifteen hours at a temperature of 1060°C. This can be the final stage unless it is necessary to apply on-glaze paint and if this happens it then has to be fired once more.

We are now in possession of the prototype which has to be given the final seal of approval before it goes into production and then into homes throughout the world to give pleasure for many years to come.

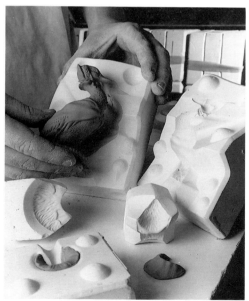

Jemima Puddle-Duck being removed from the plaster of Paris mould

Beatrix Potter figures coming out of the kiln

Decorating Beatrix Potter figures

BEATRIX POTTER

THE Peter Rabbit books written and illustrated by the late Beatrix Potter, and published by Frederick Warne & Co. Ltd., Chandos House, Bedford Court, Bedford Street, London, W.C.2, are today among the world's best sellers. Peter Rabbit, and all the other quaint characters, are known and loved by children everywhere.

John Beswick Ltd., Gold Street Works, Longton, Staffs, have the sole right of producing these figures in pottery by arrangement with the publishers. They were first made towards the end of 1948, the original models being faithfully reproduced from the illustrations in the books.

Today the following figures are being made, and more are being modelled:

1092	Jemima Puddleduck.
1098	Peter Rabbit.
1100	Tom Kitten.
1101	Timmy Tiptoes.
1102	Squirrel Nutkin.
1103	Mrs. Tittlemouse.
1104	Little Pig Robinson.
1105	Benjamin Bunny.
1106	Samuel Whiskers.
1107	Tiggy Winkle.
1108	Tailor of Gloucester.
1109	Timmie Willie.
1157	Jeremy Fisher.
1183	Lady Mouse.

Jemima Puddleduck, Samuel Whiskers, Jeremy Fisher, Peter Rabbit and Mrs. Tittlemouse seem to be watching (although with an air of dignified condescension) various stages in the manufacturing process which are shown on the opposite page

The figures appeal immediately to all admirers of the Beatrix Potter books and there is a great demand for them in Canada, the U.S.A., Mexico, Australia, New Zealand, Rhodesia, British West Africa, and Sweden. That they cannot be bought in the land in which they are made is almost an ironical paradox—Peter Rabbit fans in Britain wait eagerly for the day when they are released to the home market.

An American lady customer recently wrote to the firm: 'They are perfect because they are exactly like the original illustrations; no one has tried to improve them or add their own ideas. To my mind that exactly describes these works of art that you have produced with such fidelity for Beatrix Potter's admirers who are legion.'

It is a great tribute to all concerned with the production of the figures that during the process of transition from the pages of the books via the hands of the model makers, the mould makers, the kiln overseers, and the paintresses their charm and individuality has, if anything, been enhanced.

Reprinted from 'Pottery & Glass', June 1950

A Beatrix Potter article in 'Pottery & Glass' magazine, June 1950.

COLLECTING BEATRIX POTTER FIGURES

SAL CASTILLO

THERE is nothing more rewarding for a collector than something which pleases his or her imagination and this is why the delightful characters created by Beatrix Potter have such wide appeal. For many, turning the pages of her little books brings childhood memories flooding back and it is often these comfortable feelings of familiarity which have inspired adults to collect her work, whether it be first editions of her books, watercolours or character figures.

When the John Beswick pottery began making figures based on the original Beatrix Potter illustrations, collectors immediately welcomed the idea. It was as if the modeller had pulled something out of our imaginations, a piece of wonderful memory, and made it into something tangible. The initial collection of models was an instant success and since then Beatrix Potter fans all over the world have eagerly awaited the annual introductions. Even people not brought up with the Beatrix Potter books have fallen for the charm of the Beswick models.

Some of the earliest collections have now been handed down from one generation to another. Parents, grandparents and other relatives frequently

Display stand featuring a collection of discontinued and gold backstamp figures Pig-Wig, Simpkin, Little Pig Robinson, Mr Benjamin Bunny, and Ginger

Rare Jemima Puddle-Duck plaque

build collections for younger members of the family and sometimes they have such fun finding new pieces that they start collecting for themselves as well. Certainly it would not be wise to keep the rarer discontinued pieces in the children's room so a special Beatrix Potter china cabinet is often justified on these grounds!

The figure of *Duchess* holding a bunch of flowers (P1355) was the first to be withdrawn and it is very difficult to find today. It has only occasionally come up for sale at auction with a price tag reflecting its extreme rarity. Collectors who purchased *Duchess* at its 1967 retail price of ten shillings can consider themselves very lucky! This model should not be confused with the later version of *Duchess* holding a pie (P2601) which is not as rare, although it is still very collectable, because it was only made for four years before being withdrawn in 1983. To date 42 Beatrix Potter figures have been discontinued and some of the 1980s withdrawals have now increased in value by around twenty times their last retail price.

Knowledgeable Beatrix Potter collectors have also been seeking out the early model and colour variations, most of which have gold backstamps, and so prices are generally considerably higher for these pieces. Since 1989, when the brand name was changed from John Beswick to Royal Albert for all the models in current production, there has also been an increased demand for older pieces marked with the various brown Beswick backstamps.

There has been a noticeable surge of interest in Beatrix Potter figures in the last few years, helped no doubt by the publication of the *Beswick Collectors Handbook* in 1986, which listed all the models. There are also many avid collectors in the Beswick Collectors Circle, who swap notes about rare variations and this growing awareness has led to rapid escalation of some prices on the secondary market. Undoubtedly some collectors are excited about the investment potential of the rarer figures and this all adds to their enjoyment of their collections.

As well as the figures, there are also some related Beatrix Potter items to look out for, including the three rare plaques modelled in the shape of *Jemima Puddle-Duck* (P2082), *Peter Rabbit* (P2083) and *Tom Kitten* (P2085) which were discontinued in 1969 after only a couple of years in production. More recently there have been three relief modelled plaques, depicting scenes from the books, which were not a commercial success and so will become increasingly difficult to find in the future, in

Royal Albert wall plates and nursery clock

particular the last one depicting *Mrs Tittlemouse* (P2865). The Beatrix Potter tableware is still available in the current range and in some cases is used to enhance collections of figures — the wall plates are particularly

Jemima Puddle-Duck and Foxy Whiskered Gentleman plaque

effective as display accessories.

The market for Beatrix Potter figures continues to expand as indicated by the increasing number of annual introductions — in 1992 collectors had a choice of six new models instead of an average of three or four during the 1980s. There was also lots of activity in 1993 when Peter Rabbit celebrated his hundredth birthday. A new large

29

size figure of Peter Rabbit was launched with a commemorative Beswick backstamp and this proved so popular that more large size figures have followed.

An animated film series of Beatrix Potter tales was commissioned by Frederick Warne at a cost of 11 million pounds and there were centenary exhibitions and events in many parts of the world. Perhaps one day there will be another TV screening for the fascinating TV documentary about Beatrix Potter's life which inspired one particular American couple to start collecting six years ago. They now have more than 140 Beatrix Potter figures, including the rare *Duchess* (P1355) and some unusual model and backstamp variations. Many other collections have started following a visit to Beatrix Potter's beloved Lake District and the resulting souvenirs and gifts spark off an enjoyable new hobby. Now that there is a comprehensive new book on the subject, no doubt even more people will become aware of the delights of Beatrix Potter figures in the future.

Rare Tom Kitten plaque.

LIST OF BEATRIX POTTER FIGURES

Introduction dates are recorded in this section and not the modelling dates which have been published in previous lists. The interval between modelling and production dates can be anything between six months and two years.

P1092 **Jemima Puddle-Duck**
From 'The Tale of Jemima Puddle-Duck'
Modelled by Arthur Gredington
Introduced: 1948   Still current

P1098 **Peter Rabbit**
From 'The Tale of Peter Rabbit'
Modelled by Arthur Gredington
Introduced: 1948   Still current

P1100 **Tom Kitten**
From 'The Tale of Tom Kitten'
Modelled by Arthur Gredington
Introduced: 1948   Still current

P1101 **Timmy Tiptoes**
From 'The Tale of Timmy Tiptoes'
Modelled by Arthur Gredington
Introduced: 1948   Still current

P1102 **Squirrel Nutkin**
From 'The Tale of Squirrel Nutkin'
Modelled by Arthur Gredington
Introduced: 1948   Still current

P1103 **Mrs Tittlemouse**
From 'The Tale of Mrs Tittlemouse'
Modelled by Arthur Gredington
Introduced: 1948   Discontinued: 1993

P1104 **Little Pig Robinson**
From 'The Tale of Little Pig Robinson'
Modelled by Arthur Gredington
Introduced: 1948   Still current

P1105 **Benjamin Bunny**
From 'The Tale of Benjamin Bunny'
Modelled by Arthur Gredington
Introduced: 1948   Still current

P1106 **Samuel Whiskers**
From 'The Roly Poly Pudding'
Modelled by Arthur Gredington
Introduced: 1948   Discontinued: 1995

P1107 **Mrs Tiggy-Winkle**
From 'The Tale of Mrs Tiggy-Winkle'
Modelled by Arthur Gredington
Introduced: 1948   Still current

P1108 **Tailor of Gloucester**
From 'The Tailor of Gloucester'
Modelled by Arthur Gredington
Introduced: 1949   Still current

P1109 **Timmy Willie**
From 'The Tale of Johnny Town-Mouse'
Modelled by Arthur Gredington
Introduced: 1949   Discontinued: 1993

P1157 **Mr Jeremy Fisher**
From 'The Tale of Mr Jeremy Fisher'
Modelled by Arthur Gredington
Introduced: 1950   Still current

P1183 **Lady Mouse**
From 'The Tailor of Gloucester'
Modelled by Arthur Gredington
Introduced: 1950   Still current

P1198 **Hunca Munca**
From 'The Tale of Two Bad Mice'
Modelled by Arthur Gredington
Introduced: 1951   Still current

P1199 **Ribby**
From 'The Pie and the Patty Pan'
Modelled by Arthur Gredington
Introduced: 1951   Still current

P1200 **Mrs Rabbit**
From 'The Tale of Peter Rabbit'
Modelled by Arthur Gredington
Introduced: 1951   Still current

P1274 **Flopsy, Mopsy and Cottontail**
From 'The Tale of Peter Rabbit'
Modelled by Arthur Gredington
Introduced: 1954   Still current

P1275 **Miss Moppet**
From 'The Story of Miss Moppet'
Modelled by Arthur Gredington
Introduced: 1954   Still current

P1276 **Johnny Town-Mouse**
From 'The Tale of Johnny Town-Mouse'
Modelled by Arthur Gredington
Introduced: 1954   Discontinued: 1993

P1277 **Foxy Whiskered Gentleman**
From 'The Tale of Jemima Puddle-D
Modelled by Arthur Gredington
Introduced: 1954   Still current

P1348 **Tommy Brock**
From 'The Tale of Mr Tod'
Modelled by Graham Orwell
Introduced: 1955   Still current

P1355 **Duchess**
From 'The Pie and the Patty Pan'
Modelled by Graham Orwell
Introduced: 1955   Discontinued: 1

P1365 **Pigling Bland**
From 'The Tale of Pigling Bland'
Modelled by Graham Orwell
Introduced: 1955   Still current

P1531 **Tree Lamp Base**
Modelled by James Hayward and
Albert Hallam
Introduced: 1958   Discontinued: 1

P1545 **The Old Woman Who Lived In A**
From 'Appley Dapply's Nursery Rhy
Modelled by Colin Melbourne
Introduced: 1959   Still current

P1675 **Goody Tiptoes**
From 'The Tale of Timmy Tiptoes'
Modelled by Arthur Gredington
Introduced: 1961   Still current

P1676 **Tabitha Twitchit**
From 'The Roly Poly Pudding'
Modelled by Arthur Gredington
Introduced: 1961   Discontinued: 1

1796 **Old Mr Brown**
From 'The Tale of Squirrel Nutkin'
Modelled by Albert Hallam
Introduced: 1963   Still current

1851 **Anna Maria**
From 'The Roly Poly Pudding'
Modelled by Albert Hallam
Introduced: 1963   Discontinued: 1983

1940 **Mr Benjamin Bunny**
From 'The Tale of Benjamin Bunny'
Modelled by Arthur Gredington
Introduced: 1965   Still current

1941 **Cecily Parsley**
From 'Appley Dapply's Nursery Rhymes'
Modelled by Arthur Gredington
Introduced: 1965   Discontinued: 1993

1942 **Mrs Flopsy Bunny**
From 'The Tale of Flopsy Bunnies'
Modelled by Arthur Gredington
Introduced: 1965   Still current

2061 **Amiable Guinea Pig**
From 'Appley Dapply's Nursery Rhymes'
Modelled by Albert Hallam
Introduced: 1967   Discontinued: 1983

2082 **Jemima Puddle-Duck plaque**
From 'The Tale of Jemima Puddle-Duck'
Modelled by Albert Hallam
Introduced: 1967   Discontinued: 1969

2083 **Peter Rabbit plaque**
From 'The Tale of Peter Rabbit'
Modelled by Graham Tongue
Introduced: 1967   Discontinued: 1969

P2085 **Tom Kitten plaque**
From 'The Tale of Tom Kitten'
Modelled by Graham Tongue
Introduced: 1967   Discontinued: 1969

P2276 **Aunt Pettitoes**
From 'The Tale of Pigling Bland'
Modelled by Albert Hallam
Introduced: 1970   Discontinued: 1993

P2284 **Cousin Ribby**
From 'The Roly Poly Pudding'
Modelled by Albert Hallam
Introduced: 1970   Discontinued: 1993

P2295 **Display Stand**
Modelled by Andrew Brindley
Introduced: 1970   Still current

P2333 **Appley Dapply**
From 'Appley Dapply's Nursery Rhymes'
Modelled by Albert Hallam
Introduced: 1971   Still current

P2334 **Pickles**
From 'The Tale of Ginger and Pickles'
Modelled by Albert Hallam
Introduced: 1971   Discontinued: 1982

P2381 **Pig-Wig**
From 'The Tale of Pigling Bland'
Modelled by Albert Hallam
Introduced: 1972   Discontinued: 1982

P2424 **Mr Alderman Ptolemy**
From 'The Tale of Jeremy Fisher'
Modelled by Graham Tongue
Introduced: 1973   Still current

P2425 **Sir Isaac Newton**
From 'The Tale of Jeremy Fisher'
Modelled by Graham Tongue
Introduced: 1973   Discontinued: 1984

P2452 **Sally Henny Penny**
From 'The Tale of Ginger and Pickles'
Modelled by Albert Hallam
Introduced: 1974   Discontinued: 1993

P2453 **Mr Jackson**
From 'The Tale of Mrs Tittlemouse'
Modelled by Albert Hallam
Introduced: 1974   Still current

P2508 **Simpkin**
From 'The Tailor of Gloucester'
Modelled by Alan Maslankowski
Introduced: 1975   Discontinued: 1983

P2509 **Mr Benjamin Bunny and Peter Rabbit**
From 'The Tale of Benjamin Bunny'
Modelled by Alan Maslankowski
Introduced: 1975   Discontinued: 1995

P2543 **Mrs Rabbit and Bunnies**
From 'The Tale of Benjamin Bunny'
Modelled by David Lyttleton
Introduced: 1976   Still current

P2544 **Tabitha Twitchit and Miss Moppet**
From 'The Tale of Tom Kitten'
Modelled by David Lyttleton
Introduced: 1976   Discontinued: 1993

P2559 **Ginger**
From 'The Tale of Ginger and Pickles'
Modelled by David Lyttleton
Introduced: 1976   Discontinued: 1982

P2560 **Poorly Peter Rabbit**
From 'The Tale of Benjamin Bunny'
Modelled by David Lyttleton
Introduced: 1977   Still current

P2584 **Hunca Munca Sweeping**
From 'The Tale of Two Bad Mice'
Modelled by David Lyttleton
Introduced: 1977   Still current

P2585 **Little Black Rabbit**
From 'Appley Dapply's Nursery Rhy
Modelled by David Lyttleton
Introduced: 1977   Still current

P2586 **Fierce Bad Rabbit**
From 'The Story of Fierce Bad Rabb
Modelled by David Lyttleton
Introduced: 1977   Still current

P2594 **Jemima Puddle-Duck and
Foxy Whiskered Gentleman plaqu**
From 'The Tale of Jemima Puddle-D
Modelled by Harry Sales and
David Lyttleton
Introduced: 1977   Discontinued: 1

P2601 **The Duchess**
From 'The Pie and the Patty Pan'
Modelled by Graham Tongue
Introduced: 1979   Discontinued: 1

P2627 **Chippy Hackee**
From 'The Tale of Timmy Tiptoes'
Modelled by David Lyttleton
Introduced: 1979   Discontinued: 1

P2628 **Mr Drake Puddle-Duck**
From 'The Tale of Tom Kitten'
Modelled by David Lyttleton
Introduced: 1979   Still current

647 Rebeccah Puddle-Duck
From 'The Tale of Tom Kitten'
Modelled by David Lyttleton
Introduced: 1981   Still current

650 Peter Rabbit plaque
From 'The Tale of Peter Rabbit'
Modelled by Harry Sales and
David Lyttleton
Introduced: 1979   Discontinued: 1983

668 Thomasina Tittlemouse
From 'The Tale of Flopsy Bunnies'
Modelled by David Lyttleton
Introduced: 1981   Discontinued: 1989

685 Mrs Tittlemouse plaque
From 'The Tale of Mrs Tittlemouse'
Modelled by Harry Sales
Introduced: 1982   Discontinued: 1984

713 Diggory Diggory Delvet
From 'Appley Dapply's Nursery Rhymes'
Modelled by David Lyttleton
Introduced: 1982   Still current

716 Susan
From 'The Tale of Little Pig Robinson'
Modelled by David Lyttleton
Introduced: 1983   Discontinued: 1989

767 Old Mr Pricklepin
From 'Appley Dapply's Nursery Rhymes'
Modelled by David Lyttleton
Introduced: 1983   Discontinued: 1989

803 Benjamin Bunny Sat on a Bank
From 'The Tale of Benjamin Bunny'
Modelled by David Lyttleton
Introduced: 1983   Still current

804 The Old Woman Who Lived in a Shoe
Knitting
From 'Appley Dapply's Nursery Rhymes'
Modelled by David Lyttleton
Introduced: 1983   Still current

P2823 Jemima Puddle-Duck Made a Feather
Nest
From 'The Tale of Jemima Puddle-Duck'
Modelled by David Lyttleton
Introduced: 1983   Still current

P2877 Mrs Tiggy-Winkle Takes Tea
From 'The Tale of Mrs Tiggy-Winkle'
Modelled by David Lyttleton
Introduced: 1985   Still current

P2878 Cottontail
From 'Appley Dapply's Nursery Rhymes'
Modelled by David Lyttleton
Introduced: 1985   Discontinued: 1996

P2956 Old Mr Bouncer
From 'The Tale of Mr Tod'
Modelled by David Lyttleton
Introduced: 1986   Discontinued: 1995

P2957 Goody and Timmy Tiptoes
From 'The Tale of Timmy Tiptoes'
Modelled by David Lyttleton
Introduced: 1986   Discontinued: 1996

P2959 Old Mr Brown character jug
From 'The Tale of Squirrel Nutkin'
Modelled by Graham Tongue
Introduced: 1987   Discontinued: 1992

P2960 Mr Jeremy Fisher character jug
From 'The Tale of Mr Jeremy Fisher'
Modelled by Graham Tongue
Introduced: 1987   Discontinued: 1992

P2965 John Joiner
From 'The Roly Poly Pudding'
Modelled by Graham Tongue
Introduced: 1990   Still current

P2966 Mother Ladybird
From 'The Tale of Mrs Tittlemouse'
Modelled by Warren Platt
Introduced: 1989   Discontinued: 1996

P2971   **Babbitty Bumble**
From 'The Tale of Mrs Tittlemouse'
Modelled by Warren Platt
Introduced: 1989   Discontinued: 1993

P2989   **Tom Thumb**
From 'The Tale of Two Bad Mice'
Modelled by Warren Platt
Introduced: 1987   Still current

P2996   **Timmy Willie Sleeping**
From 'The Tale of Johnny Town-Mouse'
Modelled by Graham Tongue
Introduced: 1986   Discontinued: 1996

P3006   **Peter Rabbit character jug**
From 'The Tale of Peter Rabbit'
Modelled by Graham Tongue
Introduced: 1987   Discontinued: 1992

P3030   **Tom Kitten and Butterfly**
From 'The Tale of Tom Kitten'
Modelled by Ted Chawner
Introduced: 1987   Discontinued: 1994

P3031   **Little Pig Robinson Spying**
From 'The Tale of Little Pig Robinson'
Modelled by Ted Chawner
Introduced: 1987   Discontinued: 1993

P3088   **Jemima Puddle-Duck character jug**
From 'The Tale of Jemima Puddle-Duck'
Modelled by Ted Chawner
Introduced: 1989   Discontinued: 1992

P3090   **Mr Jeremy Fisher Digging**
From 'The Tale of Jeremy Fisher'
Modelled by Ted Chawner
Introduced: 1988   Discontinued: 1994

P3091   **Mr Tod**
From 'The Tale of Mr Tod'
Modelled by Ted Chawner
Introduced: 1988   Discontinued: 1993

P3094   **Johnny Town-Mouse with Bag**
From 'The Tale of Johnny Town-Mou
Modelled by Ted Chawner
Introduced: 1988   Discontinued: 1

P3102   **Mrs Tiggy-Winkle character jug**
From 'The Tale of Mrs Tiggy-Winkle
Modelled by Ted Chawner
Introduced: 1988   Discontinued: 1

P3103   **Tom Kitten character jug**
From 'The Tale of Tom Kitten'
Modelled by Ted Chawner
Introduced: 1989   Discontinued: 1

P3157   **Peter Rabbit in the Gooseberry**
From 'The Tale of Peter Rabbit'
Modelled by David Lyttleton
Introduced: 1989   Discontinued: 1

P3193   **Jemima Puddle-Duck and
Foxy Whiskered Gentleman**
From 'The Tale of Jemima Puddle-D
Modelled by Ted Chawner
Introduced: 1990   Still current

P3197   **Mittens and Moppet**
From 'The Tale of Tom Kitten'
Modelled by Ted Chawner
Introduced: 1990   Discontinued: 1

P3200   **Gentleman Mouse Made a Bow**
From 'The Tailor of Gloucester'
Modelled by Ted Chawner
Introduced: 1990   Discontinued: 1

P3219   **Foxy Reading Country News**
From 'The Tale of Jemima Puddle-D
Modelled by Amanda Hughes-Lubec
Introduced: 1990   Still current

P3220   **Lady Mouse Made a Curtsey**
From 'The Tailor of Gloucester'
Modelled by Amanda Hughes-Lubec
Introduced: 1990   Still current

234 **Benjamin Wakes Up**
From 'The Tale of Flopsy Bunnies'
Modelled by Amanda Hughes-Lubeck
Introduced: 1991   Still current

242 **Peter and the Red Pocket Handkerchief**
From 'The Tale of Benjamin Bunny'
Modelled by Martyn Alcock
Introduced: 1991   Still current

251 **Miss Dormouse**
From 'The Tale of Ginger and Pickles'
Modelled by Martyn Alcock
Introduced: 1991   Discontinued: 1995

252 **Pigling Eats His Porridge**
From 'The Tale of Pigling Bland'
Modelled by Martyn Alcock
Introduced: 1991   Discontinued: 1994

257 **Christmas Stocking**
From 'The Tale of Two Bad Mice'
Modelled by Martyn Alcock
Introduced: 1991   Discontinued: 1994

278 **Mrs Rabbit Cooking**
From 'The Tale of Peter Rabbit'
Modelled by Martyn Alcock
Introduced: 1992   Still current

280 **Ribby and the Patty Pan**
From 'The Pie and the Patty Pan'
Modelled by Martyn Alcock
Introduced: 1992   Still current

P3288 **Hunca Munca Spills the Beads**
From 'The Tale of Two Bad Mice'
Modelled by Martyn Alcock
Introduced: 1992   Discontinued: 1996

P3317 **Benjamin Ate a Lettuce Leaf**
From 'The Tale of Benjamin Bunny'
Modelled by Martyn Alcock
Introduced: 1992   Still current

P3319 **And This Pig Had None**
From 'Cecily Parsley's Nursery Rhymes'
Modelled by Martyn Alcock
Introduced: 1992   Still current

P3325 **No More Twist**
From 'The Tailor of Gloucester'
Modelled by Martyn Alcock
Introduced: 1992   Still current

P3473 **Peter in Bed**
From 'The Tale of Peter Rabbit'
Modelled by Martyn Alcock
Introduced: 1995   Still current

P3506 **Mr McGregor**
From 'The Tale of Peter Rabbit'
Modelled by Martyn Alcock
Introduced: 1995   Still current

P3533 **Peter Ate a Radish**
From 'The Tale of Peter Rabbit'
Modelled by Warren Platt
Introduced: 1995   Still current

LAMPS AND BOOK-ENDS

Between 1973 and 1976 the figures of *Jemima Puddle-Duck* and *Peter Rabbit* were mounted on electric lamps produced by Van Cleff Studios of Connecticut, USA. Some of the most popular figures were also mounted on wooden book-ends made by Du Toit Productions.

LARGE SIZE FIGURES

P3356   **Peter Rabbit L/S**
From 'The Tale of Peter Rabbit'
Modelled by Martyn Alcock
Introduced 1993 with Beswick backstamp
and 1994 with Royal Albert backstamp
Still current

P3372   **Mr Jeremy Fisher L/S**
From 'The Tale of Mr Jeremy Fisher'
Modelled by Martyn Alcock
Introduced: 1994   Still current

P3373   **Jemima Puddle-Duck L/S**
From 'The Tale of Jemima Puddle-Duck'
Modelled by Martyn Alcock
Introduced 1994 with Beswick backstamp
and 1995 with Royal Albert backstamp
Still current

P3398   **Mrs Rabbit L/S**
From 'The Tale of Peter Rabbit'
Modelled by Martyn Alcock
Introduced: 1994   Still current

P3403   **Benjamin Bunny L/S**
From 'The Tale of Benjamin Bunny'
Modelled by Martyn Alcock
Introduced: 1994   Still current

P3405   **Tom Kitten L/S**
From 'The Tale of Tom Kitten'
Modelled by Martyn Alcock
Introduced: 1994   Still current

P3449   **Tailor of Gloucester L/S**
From 'The Tailor of Gloucester'
Modelled by Warren Platt
Introduced: 1995   Still current

P3450   **Foxy Whiskered Gentleman L/S**
From 'The Tale of Jemima Puddle-D
Modelled by Amanda Hughes-Lubec
Introduced: 1995   Still current

Peter Rabbit in standard and large sizes.

THE BEATRIX POTTER FIGURE COLLECTION

P1092
Jemima Puddle-Duck

P1098
Peter Rabbit

P1100
Tom Kitten

P1101
Timmy Tiptoes

P1102
Squirrel Nutkin

P1103
Mrs Tittlemouse

P1104
Little Pig Robinson

P1105
Benjamin Bunny

| **P1106** | **P1107** | **P1108** | **P1109** |
| Samuel Whiskers | Mrs Tiggy-Winkle | Tailor of Gloucester | Timmy Willie |

| **P1157** | **P1183** | **P1198** | **P1199** |
| Mr Jeremy Fisher | Lady Mouse | Hunca Munca | Ribby |

40

P1200
Mrs Rabbit

P1274
Flopsy, Mopsy and
Cottontail

P1275
Miss Moppet

P1276
Johnny Town-Mouse

P1277
Foxy Whiskered Gentleman

P1348
Tommy Brock

P1355
Duchess

P1365
Pigling Bland

41

P1545
The Old Woman Who
Lived In A Shoe

P1675
Goody Tiptoes

P1676
Tabitha Twitchit

P1796
Old Mr Brown

P1851
Anna Maria

P1940
Mr Benjamin Bunny

P1941
Cecily Parsley

P1942
Mrs Flopsy Bunny

P2061
Amiable Guinea Pig

P2276
Aunt Pettitoes

P2284
Cousin Ribby

P2333
Appley Dapply

P2334
Pickles

P2381
Pig-Wig

P2424
Mr Alderman Ptolemy

P2425
Sir Isaac Newton

P2452
Sally Henny Penny

P2453
Mr Jackson

P2508
Simpkin

P2509
Mr Benjamin Bunny and
Peter Rabbit

P2543
Mrs Rabbit and Bunnies

P2544
Tabitha Twitchit and
Miss Moppet

P2559
Ginger

P2560
Poorly Peter Rabbit

| **P2584** | **P2585** | **P2586** | **P2601** |
| Hunca Munca Sweeping | Little Black Rabbit | Fierce Bad Rabbit | The Duchess |

| **P2627** | **P2628** | **P2647** | **P2668** |
| Chippy Hackee | Mr Drake Puddle-Duck | Rebeccah Puddle-Duck | Thomasina Tittlemouse |

P2713
Diggory Diggory Delvet

P2716
Susan

P2767
Old Mr Pricklepin

P2803
Benjamin Bunny
Sat on a Bank

P2804
The Old Woman Who
Lived in a Shoe, Knitting

P2823
Jemima Puddle-Duck
Made a Feather Nest

P2877
Mrs Tiggy-Winkle
Takes Tea

P2878
Cottontail

P2956
Old Mr Bouncer

P2957
Goody and Timmy Tiptoes

P2965
John Joiner

P2966
Mother Ladybird

P2971
Babbitty Bumble

P2989
Tom Thumb

P2996
Timmy Willie Sleeping

P3030
Tom Kitten and Butterfly

P3031
Little Pig Robinson Spying

P3090
Mr Jeremy Fisher Digging

P3091
Mr Tod

P3094
Johnny Town-Mouse
with Bag

P3157
Peter Rabbit in the
Gooseberry Net

P3193
Jemima Puddle-Duck and
Foxy Whiskered Gentleman

P3197
Mittens and Moppet

P3200
Gentleman Mouse
Made a Bow

P3219
Foxy Reading
Country News

P3220
Lady Mouse
Made a Curtsy

P3234
Benjamin Wakes Up

P3242
Peter and the Red Pocket
Handkerchief

P3251
Miss Dormouse

P3252
Pigling Eats His Porridge

P3257
Christmas Stocking

P3278
Mrs Rabbit Cooking

P3280
Ribby and the Patty Pan

P3288
Hunca Munca
Spills the Beads

P3317
Benjamin Ate a
Lettuce Leaf

P3319
And This Pig Had None

P3325
No More Twist

P3473
Peter in Bed

P3506
Mr McGregor

P3533
Peter Ate a Radish

P3356
Peter Rabbit
L/S

P3372
Mr Jeremy Fisher
L/S

P3373
Jemima Puddle-Duck
L/S

P3398
Mrs Rabbit
L/S

P3403
Benjamin Bunny
L/S

P3405
Tom Kitten
L/S

P3449
Tailor of Gloucester
L/S

P3450
Foxy Whiskered Gentleman
L/S

MODEL AND COLOUR VARIATIONS

LOUISE IRVINE

S OME of the Beatrix Potter figures have been in continuous production for over 40 years and during that time modelling and colouring alterations have been made for various reasons. Keen collectors have become fascinated by these variations, acquiring each different version wherever possible, and premium prices are now the norm for the rarer gold backstamp examples.

The first *Benjamin Bunny* (P1105) figure has been modified twice over the years to ease production and although the second change at the back of the hat is not immediately apparent, the removal of the projecting ears has reduced the risk of chipping. *Mr Benjamin Bunny's* arm and pipe (P1940) were remodelled in 1974 to lie against his chest so that they were also less susceptible to damage in the kiln or in transit. Similarly *Mrs Rabbit's* umbrella (P1200) is less likely to be broken in the second version where it is pressed against her dress.

As each figure is assembled by hand from separate mould parts, detailed comparisons sometimes highlight slight differences in pose, but these are

Benjamin Bunny first version (gold backstamp) and third version

Mrs Rabbit first version (gold backstamp) and second version

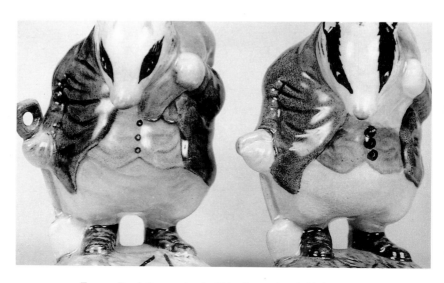

Tommy Brock first version (gold backstamp) and third version

not regarded as model alterations, for example the angle of *Lady Mouse's* mirror (P1183) can vary a little. However, the angle of *Cecily Parsley's* head (P1941) has been purposefully remodelled to face straight ahead in the second version, instead of downwards, and so looks more appealing on a display shelf. Several other changes have been made for aesthetic reasons. More interest is given to the outfits of *Little Pig Robinson* (P1104) and *Pigling Bland* (P1365) by creating a textured fabric effect on the second versions and the latter has also been rendered more attractive by changing his original sallow complexion to pale pink. *Mr Jeremy Fisher's* skin (P1157) has been modified with stripes replacing spots to more accurately reflect the original Beatrix Potter illustrations whilst *Mr Jackson* (P2453) has changed from green to brown. Differences will also be noted in the fur colours of the various squirrel and cat characters over the years.

Occasionally colour changes have been suggested by the licensing agent Copyrights who took over the management of Beatrix Potter products on behalf of Frederick Warne and Company in 1983. Their job is to ensure consistently high standards in the reproduction of the original book illustrations, whatever the medium, and they approve all the new introductions.

Cecily Parsley first and second versions

Changes in ceramic paint formulas have also caused discernible differences over the years, notably the sky-blue colour used on the original *Peter Rabbit* (P1098) has become a pale blue and the dark maroon used for *Pigling Bland's* jacket (P1365) has become a lilac shade. As each Beatrix Potter figure is hand painted there will inevitably be slight differences in interpretation from one to another, even though a factory standard is used. The painters all have different decorating techniques and often this can be seen in the painting of eyes, fur or feathers. This artistic licence is, of course, what makes individually crafted products so appealing.

Most of the model and colour variations, including new discoveries which have come to light since the first edition, are illustrated in the colour section. See pages 59 to 66.

Illustration from the 'Tale of Peter Rabbit' by Beatrix Potter.

LIST OF MODEL AND COLOUR VARIATIONS

Most of the model and colour variations are illustrated in the colour section. See pages 59 to 66.

1 **Mr Benjamin Bunny** (P1940) His arm and pipe were remodelled to rest on his chest in 1974. In the first model version he wears a dark maroon jacket. In the second model version he can be found with a dark maroon or a light mauve jacket.

2 **Mrs Rabbit** (P1200) The umbrella was remodelled to lie against her dress in the early 1970s.

3 **Fierce Bad Rabbit** (P2586) The feet and base of this figure were remodelled shortly after its introduction in 1977. The first version has the feet sticking out and the base tapering inwards. The second version has the feet tucked into the base, which tapers outwards.

4 **Benjamin Bunny Sat on a Bank** (P2803) His head was remodelled to look upwards in the mid 1980s.

5 **Benjamin Bunny** (P1105) There are three model versions of this figure. The arms and shoes were remodelled to lie against his jacket in 1974 and the ears were remodelled at the back of his hat in the 1980s. See also the black and white photograph in the section on **Model and Colour Variations**.

6 **Little Pig Robinson** (P1104) Her dress was remodelled with a textured finish in the early 1970s.

7 **Pigling Bland** (P1365) His waistcoat was remodelled with a textured finish and the colour of his jacket and skin were altered in the early 1970s.

8 **Tommy Brock** (P1348) There are three versions of this figure. The handle of the spade was first remodelled in the early 1970s and then again in the 1980s. See also the black and white photograph in the section on **Model and Colour Variations**.

9 **Timmy Tiptoes** (P1101) His fur was changed from red to grey and his jacket became paler in the 1980s.

10 **Mr Jeremy Fisher** (P1157) His spotted skin was changed to stripes in the mid 1980s.

11 **Tabitha Twitchit** (P1676) The stripes on her dress have been painted differently since the early 1970s, in particular the area between her pinafore straps.

12 **Peter Rabbit** (P1098) The base of the figure was lengthened to increase stability and the colours changed in the early 1980s.

13 **Mr Jackson** (P2453) His skin was changed from green to brown in the mid 1970s.

14 **Squirrel Nutkin** (P1102) The colours of his fur and nut changed in the early 1980s due to new ceramic paint formulas.

15 **Tom Kitten** (P1100) The colour of his coat changed due to new ceramic paint formulas.

16 **Miss Moppet** (P1275) The colour and markings on her fur became lighter in the late 1970s due to new ceramic paint formulas and different painter's styles of decoration. Current models have pronounced dark stripes.

17 **Mrs Tiggy-Winkle** (P1107) The method of painting the pattern on her dress changed during the 1970s. The first version has lots of large flowers and spots on her dress as well as prominent bristles on her bonnet. The second version has fewer, smaller flowers and less bristles on her bonnet. Occasionally examples are found with no flowers, only spots, and no bristles.

18 **Sir Isaac Newton** (P2425) The size and colouring of this figure varies. The smaller model has a dark coat and striped scarf whilst the larger model, which is about $^1/_4$ inch (0.5cm) bigger all over, has a light coat and spotted scarf.

19 **Susan** (P2716) The size and colouring of this figure varies. The smaller model has a dark blue dress whilst the larger model, which is about $^1/_4$ inch (0.5cm) bigger all over, has a light blue dress.

20 **Flopsy, Mopsy and Cottontail** (P1274) The colouring of this figure has altered over the years. In the first version, the rabbits have orange jackets. These changed to dark pink in the early 1970s and pale pink in the late 1980s.

21 **Hunca Munca Sweeping** (P2584) Early versions of this figure have a distinct daisy pattern on the dress, later versions have dots.

22 **Goody Tiptoes** (P1675) The colouring of this figure has altered over the years. In the first version, the dress is pale pink with a pattern. This was changed to a darker, plain pink in the early 1970s.

23 **Aunt Pettitoes** (P2276) The colouring of this figure has altered over the years. In the first version, the dress is pale blue and the bonnet has pale dots. These were changed to a much stronger blue in the early 1970s. The handle of the bucket also varies in size.

24 **Cecily Parsley** (P1941) The angle of her head was changed in the mid 1980s. (See page 55)

DECORATION COMPARISONS

As mentioned in the introduction, the decoration of each figure varies slightly depending on the artist involved. The following figures were painted in the same period yet have obvious differences.

25 **Amiable Guinea Pig** (P2061) Both these figures were painted in the mid 1970s yet one is much darker than the other.

26 **Old Mr Brown** (P1796) Both these figures were painted in the 1970s yet in one the squirrel is brown and in the other, orange.

27 **Mr Jeremy Fisher Digging** (P3090) Both these figures were painted in the late 1980s yet one has pronounced skin markings and the other has not.

MODEL AND COLOUR VARIATIONS
See List on Page 57

1A	1B	1C
Mr Benjamin Bunny	Mr Benjamin Bunny	Mr Benjamin Bunny
(first version)	(second version)	(second version)
	maroon jacket	mauve jacket

2A	2B	3A	3B
Mrs Rabbit	Mrs Rabbit	Fierce Bad Rabbit	Fierce Bad Rabbit
(first version)	(second version)	(first version)	(second version)

4A	4B	5A	5B
Benjamin Bunny	Benjamin Bunny	Benjamin Bunny	Benjamin Bunny
Sat on a Bank	Sat on a Bank	(first version)	(second version)
(first version)	(second version)		

6A	6B	7A	7B
Little Pig Robinson	Little Pig Robinson	Pigling Bland	Pigling Bland
(first version)	(second version)	(first version)	(second version)

8A	8B	9A	9B
Tommy Brock	Tommy Brock	Timmy Tiptoes	Timmy Tiptoes
(first version)	(second version)	(first version)	(second version)

10A	10B	11A	11B
Mr Jeremy Fisher	Mr Jeremy Fisher	Tabitha Twitchit	Tabitha Twitchit
(first version)	(second version)	(first version)	(second version)

12A	12B	13A	13B
Peter Rabbit	Peter Rabbit	Mr Jackson	Mr Jackson
(first version)	(second version)	(first version)	(second version)

14A	14B
Squirrel Nutkin	Squirrel Nutkin
(first version)	(second version)

15A	15B
Tom Kitten	Tom Kitten
(first version)	(second version)

16A Miss Moppet (first version)	16B Miss Moppet (second version)	16C Miss Moppet (third version)

17A Mrs Tiggywinkle (first version)	17B Mrs Tiggywinkle (second version) with no bristles	17C Mrs Tiggywinkle (second version)

18A	18B	19A	19B
Sir Isaac Newton	Sir Isaac Newton	Susan	Susan
(first version)	(second version)	(first version)	(second version)

20A	20B	20C
Flopsy, Mopsy and Cottontail	Flopsy, Mopsy and Cottontail	Flopsy, Mopsy and Cottontail
(first version)	(second version)	(third version)

21A
Hunca Munca Sweeping
(first version)

21B
Hunka Munca Sweeping
(second version)

22A
Goody Tiptoes
(first version)

22B
Goody Tiptoes
(second version)

23A
Aunt Pettitoes
(first version)

23B
Aunt Pettitoes
(second version)

25A
Amiable Guinea Pig
(dark jacket)

25B
Amiable Guinea Pig
(light jacket)

26A	26B	27A	27B
Old Mr Brown (dark colour)	Old Mr Brown (light colour)	Mr Jeremy Fisher digging (with spots)	Mr Jeremy Fisher digging (without spots)

Harry Sales' drawing for Beatrix Potter resin figure.

MODELLERS AND DESIGNERS

VALERIE BAYNTON

ARTHUR Gredington was a talented modeller who studied at the Royal College of Art in London. He joined Beswick in 1939 as the first resident modeller. In 1947 he created the first Beatrix Potter figure, *Jemima Puddle-Duck* (P1092) and, following the success of this, modelled 25 more characters during the 1950s and 60s. Other work by him was varied but notable are his meticulous sculptures of named animals such as *Bois Russell*, winner of the 1938 Derby. Arthur Gredington retired in 1968 and died in 1971.

James Hayward spent the greater part of his working life at Beswick, joining the company in 1926, aged 16, and retiring in 1975. From 1934, he was responsible for designing the decorative treatments for all Beswick products, including vases, animals and tableware. His particular concern, when creating decorations for the Beatrix Potter characters, was to reflect the colours and shades used in Miss Potter's original illustrations. James Hayward was a man of exceptional calibre — he was a superb glaze chemist, a talented artist and designer and he motivated and inspired the people working for him.

Graham Orwell was briefly employed at Beswick from 1954 to 1955. However, during this period he modelled both character and naturalistic animals. He contributed three models to the collection, the now rare first model of *Duchess* (P1355), *Tommy Brock* (P1348) and *Pigling Bland* (P1365).

Colin Melbourne was at Beswick for just under two years from 1956 to 1958. He designed a new ornamental collection called the 'CM' series but also contributed one Beatrix Potter subject *The Old Woman Who Lived In A Shoe* (P1545). His career since 1958 has been varied and he was the first principal of the Sir Henry Doulton School of Sculpture in Stoke-on-Trent.

Albert Hallam joined Beswick in 1926 as an apprentice mould-maker and he made many of the production moulds for the early Beatrix Potter figures. During the 1950s he became a modeller and his work included several Beatrix Potter subjects such as the *Amiable Guinea Pig* (P2061) and *Anna Maria* (P1851). He retired in 1975 and, sadly, died within a year.

Harry Sales joined Beswick in 1960 as assistant to James Hayward and he was appointed Design Manager in 1975. He was responsible for the design and development of the Beatrix Potter figures for many years and he produced detailed drawings for the modellers to work from. The wall plaques were also his designs as were the Studio Sculptures in bonded ceramic. Since 1986 he has worked as a freelance designer.

David Lyttleton specialised in character animal studies, such as the Beatrix Potter collection and Kitty McBride's mice. Models by him include *Tabitha Twitchit and Miss Moppet* (P2544) and *Hunca Munca Sweeping* (P2584). He worked at Beswick from 1973 until 1986.

Alan Maslankowski worked for a long period as a freelance modeller but he is now a resident figure sculptor at Royal Doulton. From 1973 to 1976, he was commissioned by Beswick to produce a variety of models including two characters for the Beatrix Potter collection — *Simpkin* (P2508) and *Mr Benjamin Bunny and Peter Rabbit* (P2509).

Ted Chawner was originally employed at Beswick as a character jug painter but he also had modelling talents and for two years helped in the design studios. He contributed several Beatrix Potter studies to the collection, including *Little Pig Robinson Spying* (P3031), and he left in 1990 to establish his own business in Scotland.

Graham Tongue has worked for the company since 1966 and his range of work has been extensive and varied. His sculptures have included birds of prey and race horses as well as figures for the Beatrix Potter collection, such as *Timmy Willie Sleeping* (P2996), and the first three character jugs. As Design Manager from 1986 to 1995, he provided detailed designs for most of the Beatrix Potter figures which were modelled by the Beswick studio team. He now models for Royal Doulton from his own studio.

Peter Roberts has worked for the company since 1966 and in 1989 was appointed Art Director. He has been involved with tableware design particularly for Royal Albert. He supervised the development of the Beatrix Potter gift ware collection.

The Beswick Studios Today

There are three modellers working on the Beatrix Potter collection at the studio today, Amanda Hughes-Lubeck, Warren Platt and Martyn Alcock. They are all involved in a variety of projects and do not specialise solely in one area.

Warren Platt joined the studios in 1985 and was responsible for the unusual studies of Beatrix Potter's insect characters, *Mother Ladybird* (P2966) and *Babbitty Bumble* (P2971). He also likes creating natural bird and wildlife studies such as *The Chaffinch* and *The Hare*.

Martyn Alcock joined the studios in 1986 and has modelled many of the more recent Beatrix Potter figures, for example *Peter and the Red Pocket Handkerchief* (P3242). His other work includes birds such as *The Blue Tit* and *The Wren*.

Amanda Hughes-Lubeck studied at the Sir Henry Doulton School of Sculpture before joining the studio in 1988. She particularly likes modelling animals, such as otters and horses, but also enjoys creating characters for the Beatrix Potter collection. *Lady Mouse Made a Curtsey* (P3220) is one of her models. In 1995 she was appointed Design Studio Head at Beswick.

Modeller Amanda Hughes-Lubeck.

Painting Beatrix Potter figures.

Pottery base for Beatrix Potter figures.

BACKSTAMPS AND DATING

LOUISE IRVINE

THIS selection of backstamps illustrates the variety of marks to be found on Beatrix Potter figures. Approximate dates of use have been deduced from studying a large number of figures and records of company name changes. Although a copyright date appears on most of the models, this only indicates the year the design was first introduced, not when a particular model was made. Figures which have been in production for many years can be found with several different backstamps and the gold varieties are generally the most sought-after by collectors. A total of 38 figures can be found with John Beswick gold backstamps and *Pig-Wig* (P2381) was the last model to be introduced with this type of mark.

Seven gold backstamps are illustrated in this section and they range in colour from a pale silvery shade to a deep rich gold. The earliest, G1, features a circular Beswick trade mark and this has only been recorded on a few models including *Peter Rabbit* (P1098), introduced in 1948, and *Johnny Town-Mouse* (P1276), introduced in 1954. The most widely used gold backstamp was G2 which appears on models introduced between 1948 and 1965. During the late 1950s and 60s, a few of the character's names were written in unusual scripts along with Beatrix Potter's name which is usually in upper case type, for example *Tommy Brock* (P1348), *Pigling Bland* (P1365) and *Tabitha Twitchit* (P1676). By 1970 the backstamp was invariably in upper or lower case type and this continued on all the brown backstamps which first appeared in 1972. The change of style took place following Royal Doulton's acquisition of the Beswick factory in 1969 and their growing influence in production from the early 1970s.

Eleven different brown backstamps are illustrated in this section and the most commonly used during the 1970s was B2. This was applied to many of the early models as stock of the old style backstamps ran out. In 1983 Frederick Warne and Company appointed a licensing company to represent their Beatrix Potter interests with all the different manufacturers who make products inspired by the books. Consequently 'Licensed by Copyrights' has been incorporated into the backstamp design since 1984.

In some parts of the world John Beswick is not a well-known brand name and so, in order to increase international recognition of the company, 'Studio of Royal Doulton' was added to the backstamp in 1988. The following year, however, the decision was made to change the brand name to Royal Albert to facilitate wider distribution. To commemorate this change in 1989, a special gold backstamp was used on six of the most popular models and no doubt these will become collectable in the future.

In 1993 Peter Rabbit celebrated his centenary and a large size figure of this character was issued with a commemorative backstamp. The following year the backstamp was changed to Royal Albert to match the rest of the range. The large size Jemima Puddle-Duck figure experienced a similar change. A different Beswick backstamp was used in 1994 only to mark the centenary of the John Beswick factory.

Occasionally there are variations in the spelling of the character's names on the backstamps, for example Tabitha Twitchit has also been spelt Tabitha Twitchett and Thomasina Tittlemouse is spelt Tomasina. Beatrix Potter's original spellings have been used throughout this book.

Some new backstamps have been discovered since the first edition of this book and these have been linked to existing marks, for example G1A and G1B.

GOLD BACKSTAMPS

G1 Gold backstamp with a *circular* Beswick mark, character's name in *italic script* and a copyright notice for F. Warne and Co Ltd. in use from 1948.

G1A Gold backstamp as G1 but the copyright notice is in *italic script* and does not include F. Warne and Co Ltd. in use from 1948. There is also a variation of this mark with the words *Beswick England* arranged in straight lines because of space limitations.

G1B Gold backstamp as G1 but with no copyright notice in use from 1948.

G4 As G2 but with Beatrix Potter and the character's name in *upper case script* in use from 1955.

G2 Gold backstamp with an *oval* Beswick mark and character's name in *italic script* in use from 1948. There is also a variation of this mark with *Copyright* in italic script.

G5 As G2 but with character's name in *different script* in use from 1961.

G3 As G2 but with the character's name in *upper case type within inverted commas* in use from 1950.

G6 As G2 but with the character's name in *lower case type* in use from 1970. There is a variation of this mark with Beatrix Potter and the character's name in *slanted* type.

G7 As G2 but with the character's name in *upper case type* used in 1971 and 1972.

G8 Gold backstamp with *Royal Albert Crown* mark to commemorate the brand name change in 1989 and used on *Peter Rabbit, Benjamin Bunny, Jemima Puddle-Duck, Hunca Munca, Flopsy, Mopsy and Cottontail, Mrs Rabbit and Bunnies.* There is a variation of this mark without the crown symbol.

TRANSITIONAL BACKSTAMP

T1 A transitional backstamp has been recorded with the name of the figure in *gold italic script* and the rest of the mark in *brown print* in use around 1972.

BROWN BACKSTAMPS

B1 Brown backstamp with BESWICK ENGLAND mark, F. Warne & Co. Ltd, copyright date, and Beatrix Potter's character name in *upper case type within inverted commas* used in 1972.

B2 Brown backstamp with Beswick ENGLAND mark, F. Warne & Co. Ltd, copyright date, and Beatrix Potter's character name in *lower case type within inverted commas* in use from 1974.

BEATRIX POTTER'S
"Sir Isaac Newton"
F. Warne & Co. Ltd.
ⓒ **Copyright** 1973
BESWICK
MADE IN ENGLAND

B3 Variation of B2 but with *MADE IN ENGLAND* used in 1973. This mark is also found without a copyright date.

BEATRIX POTTER'S
" Anna Maria "
F. Warne & Co.Ltd.
Copyright
BESWICK ENGLAND

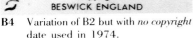

B4 Variation of B2 but with *no copyright* date used in 1974.

BEATRIX POTTER'S
Chippy Hackee
F. Warne & Co.Ltd.
ⓒ Copyright 1979
BESWICK ENGLAND

B5 Variation of B2 but with *no inverted commas* around character's name in use from 1976.

BEATRIX POTTER'S
"Benjamin Bunny"
"Sat on a bank "
ⓒ **Frederick Warne P.L.C. 1983**
BESWICK ENGLAND

B6 As B2 but with *Frederick Warne P.L.C.* in use from 1982.

BEATRIX POTTER
" Cottontail "
ⓒ F. Warne & Co. 1985
Licensed by Copyrights
BESWICK ENGLAND

B7 Brown backstamp with BESWICK ENGLAND mark, F. Warne & Co, copyright date, *Licensed by Copyrights*, and Beatrix Potter (instead of Potter's) character name in use from 1984.

BEATRIX POTTER
"Tabitha Twitchit"
ⓒ Frederick Warne & Co. 1961
Licensed by Copyrights
BESWICK ENGLAND

B8 Variation of B7 but with *Frederick Warne & Co* in use from 1985.

BEATRIX POTTER
"Mr. Jeremy Fisher Digging"
ⓒ **F. Warne & Co. 1988**
Licensed by Copyrights
John Beswick
Studio of Royal Doulton
England

B9 Brown backstamp with *John Beswick Studio of Royal Doulton* mark, F. Warne & Co and copyright date in use from 1988.

BEATRIX POTTER
"Johnny Town-Mouse with Bag"
ⓒ Frederick Warne & Co. 1988
Licensed by Copyrights
John Beswick
Studio of Royal Doulton
England

B10 Variation of B9 but with *Frederick Warne & Co* in use from 1988.

ROYAL ALBERT ®
ENGLAND
Peter in the Gooseberry Net
Beatrix Potter
ⓒ F. WARNE & CO. 1989
ⓒ 1989 ROYAL ALBERT LTD

B11 Brown backstamp with *Royal Albert Crown* mark in use from 1989. There is a variation of this mark without the crown symbol.

COMMEMORATIVE BACKSTAMPS

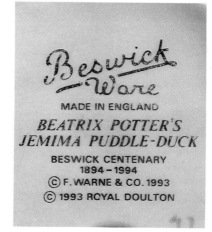

C1 For the centenary of Peter Rabbit, a new backstamp was designed for the large size model of the character. Peter Rabbit is printed in blue and brown against black type. This commemorative mark was used in 1993 only and later large size Peter Rabbit figures have the standard Royal Albert mark.

C2 For the centenary of the John Beswick factory a new backstamp was designed and used on the large size model of Jemima Puddle-Duck only. The old-style company trademark is included in this brown printed backstamp which was used in 1994 only. Later large size Jemima Puddle-Duck figures have the standard Royal Albert mark.

© F. Warne & Co., 1902, 1987

Illustration from 'The Tale of Peter Rabbit' by Beatrix Potter.

RARITY GUIDE

NICK TZIMAS

T HIS guide has been compiled in response to frequent requests from collectors and is intended to provide an indication of relative scarcity. It must be stressed that the comparative rarity of Beatrix Potter figures is a matter of opinion and these assessments are based on my personal experience of the Beatrix Potter market, particularly the dramatic developments of the last few years.

Although Beatrix Potter figures were first introduced in 1947, it was not until 20 years later that the first model was withdrawn from the range, the now extremely rare *Duchess with Flowers*. A further 11 figures were withdrawn during the 1980s but prices did not escalate until the 1990s when the market was stimulated by 30 more withdrawals and an abundance of new models, making a total of 96 figures to find. The Beatrix Potter centenary in 1993 and the publication of the first specialist book on the figures also helped to focus more attention on the buoyant collectors market.

Beatrix Potter figures now appear regularly at auction and Beswick dealers carry large stocks of discontinued models. Saleroom results and prices at antique shows and markets have been monitored and then related to purchases and collector demand to produce these estimates. Other valuation criteria include: introduction dates; production periods and factory marks.

After much deliberation, figures have been assigned one of six rarity categories. As this is a controversial subject, no doubt some collectors will have different ideas based on the elusiveness of particular models in different parts of the world. The fact that a figure has been designated 'common' need not detract from its desirability. Some of the most appealing subjects fall into this category as they were best selling models with wide aesthetic appeal. In the end rarity is determined by what collectors want and the prices they are prepared to pay, not by dealers and guides.

Note: These rarity categories are for standard figures without colour, model or gold backstamp variations.

RARITY CATEGORIES

A:	EXTREMELY RARE	D:	LESS COMMON
B:	VERY RARE	E:	COMMON
C:	RARE	F:	STILL IN PRODUCTION

BEATRIX POTTER FIGURES

P2061   Amiable Guinea Pig
Issued: 1967-1983
Rarity: C

P3319   And This Pig Had None
Issued: 1992   Still current
Rarity: F

P1851   Anna Maria
Issued: 1963-1983
Rarity: C

P2333   Appley Dapply
Issued: 1971   Still current
Rarity: Beswick: E   Royal Albert: F

P2276   Aunt Pettitoes
Issued: 1970-1993
Rarity: Beswick: E   Royal Albert: E

P2971   Babbitty Bumble
Issued: 1989-1993
Rarity: D

P3317   Benjamin Ate a Lettuce Leaf
Issued: 1992   Still current
Rarity: F

P1105   Benjamin Bunny
Issued: 1948   Still current
Rarity: Beswick: D   Royal Albert: F

P2803   Benjamin Bunny Sat on a Bank
Issued: 1983   Still current
Rarity: F

P3234   Benjamin Wakes Up
Issued: 1992   Still current
Rarity: F

P1941   Cecily Parsley
Issued: 1965-1993
Rarity: Beswick: D   Royal Albert: E

P2627   Chippy Hackee
Issued: 1979-1993
Rarity: Beswick: E   Royal Albert: E

P3257   Christmas Stocking
Issued: 1991-1994
Rarity: E

P2878   Cottontail
Issued: 1985-1996
Rarity: Beswick: E   Royal Albert: E

P2284   Cousin Ribby
Issued: 1970-1993
Rarity: Beswick: D   Royal Albert: E

P2713   Diggory Diggory Delvet
Issued: 1982   Still current
Rarity: Beswick: D   Royal Albert: E

P2295   Display Stand
Issued: 1970   Still current
Rarity: F

P1355   Duchess (With Flowers)
Issued: 1955-1967
Rarity: A

P2601   Duchess (With Pie)
Issued: 1979-1982
Rarity: C

P2586   Fierce Bad Rabbit
Issued: 1977   Still current
Rarity: Beswick: D   Royal Albert: F

P1274   Flopsy, Mopsy and Cottontail
Issued: 1954   Still current
Rarity: Beswick: D   Royal Albert: F

P3219   Foxy Reading Country News
Issued: 1990   Still current
Rarity: F

P1277   Foxy Whiskered Gentleman
Issued: 1954   Still current
Rarity: Beswick: D   Royal Albert: F

P3200   Gentleman Mouse Made a Bow
Issued: 1990-1996
Rarity: E

559 Ginger
Issued: 1976-1982
Rarity: B

957 Goody and Timmy Tiptoes
Issued: 1986-1996
Rarity: Beswick: C   Royal Albert: E

675 Goody Tiptoes
Issued: 1961   Still current
Rarity: Beswick: E   Royal Albert: F

198 Hunca Munca
Issued: 1951   Still current
Rarity: Beswick: E   Royal Albert: F

288 Hunca Munca Spills the Beads
Issued: 1992-1996
Rarity: E

584 Hunca Munca Sweeping
Issued: 1977   Still current
Rarity: Beswick: D   Royal Albert: F

092 Jemima Puddle-Duck
Issued: 1948   Still current
Rarity: Beswick: D   Royal Albert: F

088 Jemima Puddle-Duck Character Jug
Issued: 1988-1992
Rarity: Beswick: D   Royal Albert: D

082 Jemima Puddle-Duck Figure Plaque
Issued: 1967-1969
Rarity: A

193 Jemima Puddle-Duck and
Foxy Whiskered Gentleman
Issued: 1990   Still current
Rarity: F

954 Jemima Puddle-Duck and
Foxy Whiskered Gentleman Plaque
Issued: 1977-1982
Rarity: D

823 Jemima Puddle-Duck
Made a Feather Nest
Issued: 1983   Still current
Rarity: Beswick: E   Royal Albert: F

P2965 John Joiner
Issued: 1990   Still current
Rarity: F

P1276 Johnny Town-Mouse
Issued: 1954-1993
Rarity: Beswick: E   Royal Albert: E

P3094 Johnny Town-Mouse with Bag
Issued: 1988-1994
Rarity: Beswick: C   Royal Albert: D

P1183 Lady Mouse
Issued: 1950   Still current
Rarity: Beswick: D   Royal Albert: F

P3220 Lady Mouse Made a Curtsey
Issued: 1990   Still current
Rarity: F

P2585 Little Black Rabbit
Issued: 1977   Still current
Rarity: Beswick: E   Royal Albert: F

P1104 Little Pig Robinson
Issued: 1948   Still current
Rarity: Beswick: E   Royal Albert: F

P3031 Little Pig Robinson Spying
Issued: 1987-1993
Rarity: Beswick: D   Royal Albert: E

P3251 Miss Dormouse
Issued: 1991-1995
Rarity: E

P1275 Miss Moppet
Issued: 1954   Still current
Rarity: Beswick: D   Royal Albert: F

P3197 Mittens and Moppet
Issued: 1990-1994
Rarity: E

P2966 Mother Ladybird
Issued: 1989-1996
Rarity: E

P2424 Mr Alderman Ptolemy
Issued: 1973   Still current
Rarity: Beswick: D   Royal Albert: F

P1940 Mr Benjamin Bunny
Issued: 1965   Still current
Rarity: Beswick: E   Royal Albert: F

P2509 Mr Benjamin Bunny and
Peter Rabbit
Issued: 1975-1995
Rarity: Beswick: D   Royal Albert: E

P2628 Mr Drake Puddle-Duck
Issued: 1979   Still current
Rarity: Beswick: D   Royal Albert: F

P2453 Mr Jackson
Issued: 1974   Still current
Rarity: Beswick: D   Royal Albert: F

P1157 Mr Jeremy Fisher
Issued: 1950   Still current
Rarity: Beswick: D   Royal Albert: F

P3090 Mr Jeremy Fisher Digging
Issued: 1988-1994
Rarity: Beswick: C   Royal Albert: E

P2960 Mr Jeremy Fisher Character Jug
Issued: 1987-1992
Rarity: Beswick: D   Royal Albert: D

P3506 Mr McGregor
Issued: 1995   Still current
Rarity: F

P3091 Mr Tod
Issued: 1988-1993
Rarity: Beswick: B   Royal Albert: D

P1942 Mrs Flopsy Bunny
Issued: 1965   Still current
Rarity: Beswick: D   Royal Albert: F

P1200 Mrs Rabbit
Issued: 1951   Still current
Rarity: Beswick: D   Royal Albert: F

P2543 Mrs Rabbit and Bunnies
Issued: 1976   Still current
Rarity: Beswick: D   Royal Albert: F

P3278 Mrs Rabbit Cooking
Issued: 1992   Still current
Rarity: F

P1107 Mrs Tiggy-Winkle
Issued: 1948   Still current
Rarity: Beswick: E   Royal Albert: F

P2877 Mrs Tiggy-Winkle Takes Tea
Issued: 1985   Still current
Rarity: Beswick: D   Royal Albert: F

P3102 Mrs Tiggy-Winkle Character Jug
Issued: 1988-1992
Rarity: Beswick: D   Royal Albert: D

P1103 Mrs Tittlemouse
Issued: 1948-1993
Rarity: Beswick: D   Royal Albert: E

P2685 Mrs Tittlemouse Plaque
Issued: 1982-1984
Rarity: C

P3325 No More Twist
Issued: 1992   Still current
Rarity: F

P2956 Old Mr Bouncer
Issued: 1986-1995
Rarity: Beswick: E   Royal Albert: F

P1796 Old Mr Brown
Issued: 1963   Still current
Rarity: Beswick: E   Royal Albert: F

P2959 Old Mr Brown Character Jug
Issued: 1987-1992
Rarity: Beswick: D   Royal Albert: D

P2767 Old Mr Pricklepin
Issued: 1983-1989
Rarity: Beswick: D   Royal Albert: C

P1545 Old Woman Who Lived In a Shoe
Issued: 1959   Still current
Rarity: Beswick: E   Royal Albert: F

304   Old Woman Who Lived In a Shoe Knitting
Issued: 1983   Still current
Rarity: Beswick: C   Royal Albert: F

242   Peter and the Red Pocket Handkerchief
Issued: 1991   Still current
Rarity: F

533   Peter Ate a Radish
Issued: 1995   Still current
Rarity: F

473   Peter in Bed
Issued: 1995   Still current
Rarity: F

098   Peter Rabbit
Issued: 1948   Still current
Rarity: Beswick: D   Royal Albert: F

006   Peter Rabbit Character Jug
Issued: 1987-1992
Rarity: Beswick: D   Royal Albert: D

083   Peter Rabbit Figure Plaque
Issued: 1967-1969
Rarity: A

650   Peter Rabbit Plaque
Issued: 1979-1983
Rarity: D

157   Peter Rabbit in the Gooseberry Net
Issued: 1989-1995
Rarity: E

334   Pickles
Issued: 1971-1982
Rarity: C

381   Pig-Wig
Issued: 1972-1982
Rarity: C

P1365   Pigling Bland
Issued: 1955   Still current
Rarity: Beswick: D   Royal Albert: F

P3252   Pigling Eats His Porridge
Issued: 1991-1994
Rarity: E

P2560   Poorly Peter Rabbit
Issued: 1976   Still current
Rarity: Beswick: D   Royal Albert: F

P2647   Rebeccah Puddle-Duck
Issued: 1981   Still current
Rarity: Beswick: D   Royal Albert: F

P1199   Ribby
Issued: 1951   Still current
Rarity: Beswick: D   Royal Albert: F

P3280   Ribby and the Patty Pan
Issued: 1992   Still current
Rarity: F

P2452   Sally Henny Penny
Issued: 1974-1993
Rarity: Beswick: E   Royal Albert: E

P1106   Samuel Whiskers
Issued: 1948-1995
Rarity: Beswick: E   Royal Albert: E

P2508   Simpkin
Issued: 1975-1983
Rarity: B

P2425   Sir Isaac Newton
Issued: 1973-1984
Rarity: C

P1102   Squirrel Nutkin
Issued: 1948   Still current
Rarity: Beswick: E   Royal Albert: F

P2716   Susan
Issued: 1983-1989
Rarity: Beswick: C   Royal Albert: C

P1676   Tabitha Twitchit
Issued: 1961-1995
Rarity: Beswick: **D**   Royal Albert: **E**

P2544   Tabitha Twitchit and Miss Moppet
Issued: 1976-1993
Rarity: Beswick: **D**   Royal Albert: **E**

P1108   Tailor of Gloucester
Issued: 1949   Still current
Rarity: Beswick: **E**   Royal Albert: **F**

P2668   Thomasina Tittlemouse
Issued: 1981-1989
Rarity: Beswick: **D**   Royal Albert: **C**

P1101   Timmy Tiptoes
Issued: 1948   Still current
Rarity: Beswick: **E**   Royal Albert: **F**

P1109   Timmy Willie
Issued: 1949-1993
Rarity: Beswick: **E**   Royal Albert: **E**

P2996   Timmy Willie Sleeping
Issued: 1986-1996
Rarity: **E**

P1100   Tom Kitten
Issued: 1948   Still current
Rarity: Beswick: **D**   Royal Albert: **F**

P3103   Tom Kitten Character Jug
Issued: 1989-1992
Rarity: Beswick: **D**   Royal Albert: **D**

P3030   Tom Kitten and Butterfly
Issued: 1987-1994
Rarity: Beswick: **C**   Royal Albert: **E**

P2085   Tom Kitten Figure Plaque
Issued: 1967-1969
Rarity: **A**

P2989   Tom Thumb
Issued: 1987   Still current
Rarity: Beswick: **D**   Royal Albert: **F**

P1348   Tommy Brock
Issued: 1955   Still current
Rarity: Beswick: **D**   Royal Albert: **F**

P1531   Tree Lamp Base
Issued: 1958-1982
Rarity: **C**

LARGE SIZE FIGURES

P3403   Benjamin Bunny
Issued: 1994   Still current
Rarity: **F**

P3450   Foxy Whiskered Gentleman
Issued: 1995   Still current
Rarity: **F**

P3373   Jemima Puddle-Duck
Issued: 1994   Still current
Rarity: **F**

P3372   Jeremy Fisher
Issued: 1994   Still current
Rarity: **F**

P3398   Mrs Rabbit
Issued: 1994   Still current
Rarity: **F**

P3356   Peter Rabbit
Issued: 1994   Still current
Rarity: **F**

P3449   Tailor of Gloucester
Issued: 1995   Still current
Rarity: **F**

P3405   Tom Kitten
Issued: 1994   Still current
Rarity: **F**

BEATRIX POTTER SERIES WARE

LOUISE IRVINE

IN THE early 1900s Charles Noke, the Art Director of Royal Doulton, developed a new range of gift items which he called Series Ware. Taking an assortment of stock shapes, including functional and ornamental designs, he decorated them with a host of characters from literature and legend. Each shape featured a different scene and the idea was to collect every one in the series, hence the name. Dickens and Shakespeare provided lots of suitable subject matter for adult gifts whilst the children's classic *Alice's Adventures in Wonderland* inspired designs for a younger audience.

Sadly, at that time, the charming illustrations from Beatrix Potter's new books were not available for reproduction in the UK as the rights had been sold to a German manufacturer. Miss Potter was not pleased with their interpretation of her books, finding the resulting teaset very ugly. An Army and Navy catalogue of 1907 illustrates the German range which included six different subjects depicted on a variety of items. The First World War released Beatrix Potter from the German contract and Grimwade's of Stoke-on-Trent immediately sought permission to produce a new range of nursery ware featuring illustrations from her books. The launch was delayed until 1922 because of war-time shortages but, although critical of the long development period, Miss Potter was very pleased with the final results. Production must have been limited as the Grimwade designs are not easy to find and premium prices are paid for these desirable 1920s pieces.

In 1949 Wedgwood received permission to create a range of nursery ware featuring Peter Rabbit, the hero of Miss Potter's first book, and these designs have been in production ever since. However, the Royal Doulton group also became interested in producing some Beatrix Potter nursery and gift ware, given their long term success with figures, and in 1987 Frederick Warne granted a licence which enabled them to reproduce all the characters from the books except Peter Rabbit. Designers at the company's Royal Albert studio were given the task of interpreting the Beatrix Potter illustrations for the new collection.

For nearly a hundred years, the Royal Albert factory has specialised in fine bone china tableware and their *Old Country Roses* design is the world's best selling pattern. In 1964 Royal Albert became part of the Royal Doulton group and the studio continues to specialise in traditional designs with elaborate fluted and embossed shapes. Design Director Peter Roberts has

Peter Roberts

more than 30 years experience with Royal Albert and he chose the best shapes for the Beatrix Potter scenes and sensitively adapted the illustrations to fit. A very talented designer, Peter has worked on many nursery and gift ware ranges for the Royal Doulton group, including the *Brambly Hedge* and *Snowman* collections, and he is always sympathetic to the style of the original illustrators.

Two distinct styles of ware were produced for the launch collection, entitled *The World of Beatrix Potter*. For children's meal-times, a range of simple, practical bone china shapes was developed with scenes from favourite tales, such as *Benjamin Bunny, Tom Kitten, Jemima Puddle-Duck* and *Jeremy Fisher*. The name of the book is featured prominently in the overall design and the border characters, who read or carry books, were derived from Beatrix Potter's endpapers for *The Tale of Peter Rabbit*. The same border characters feature prominently in the presentation boxes which were developed for gift occasions. The two piece baby set features a robust baby plate and two handled hug-a-mug whilst the three piece children's set includes a one handled hug-a-mug, cereal bowl and plate.

More ornate designs were created for decorative purposes. Different episodes from the tales of *Benjamin Bunny, Jemima Puddle-Duck* and *Jeremy Fisher* were all set in detailed landscape borders for a collection of square wall plates. These remained in production until 1993 by which time they had been superceded by the large Gainsborough plate which was suitable for either display or practical use. The Gainsborough shape, with its embossed rim and rococo details, has been popular in the Royal Albert range for a number of years. Although still functional, it has a decorative look which is ideal for the Beatrix Potter range as many collectors like to display the plates and teawares alongside their figures. Different scenes can be found on the diverse shapes, in the manner of Series Ware, and committed collectors look out for all the variations. In 1989 a teapot, sugar and cream joined the cups, saucers, beakers, plates and coasters and no doubt there will be more new shapes in the future.

Beatrix Potter nursery ware

Each scene on the Gainsborough shape is framed with a border of wild flowers, specially designed to suit the character. Thus Jeremy Fisher has water lilies and other aquatic plants and Benjamin Bunny has pinks interspersed with radish leaves. These designs were the work of Peter Roberts and his freelance assistant Glennys Corker. Together they chose the most appropriate illustrations from the books and re-drew them, modifying the backgrounds to suit the shape and colours in order to gain the best possible reproduction from the litho printing process. Their interpretation is thoroughly scrutinised by Copyrights, who license all the Beatrix Potter merchandise on behalf of Frederick Warne.

As much consideration is given to the complex design for a nursery clock as to the tiny motif for an eggcup or key fob. Six different key fob designs were introduced in 1989 but they only remained in production until 1990 so they are increasingly difficult to find. Also elusive today are the Beatrix Potter florals which were produced between 1987 and 1992 in conjunction with expert flower makers at the company's Royal Adderley studios. Miniature containers appropriate to the character were chosen, for example the tea kettle for Mrs Tiggywinkle and the garden watering can for Peter Rabbit. This is the only instance of Peter Rabbit appearing in the Royal Albert range as florals are classified differently from nursery ware in merchandising agreements so it does not encroach upon the Wedgwood contract.

The majority of the Royal Albert range is still in current production so designs are easily obtainable, whether they are for decorating a child's nursery or accessorising an adult collection. No doubt there will continue to be new introductions on a regular basis, giving even more scope for collecting Beatrix Potter Series Ware in the future.

Beatrix Potter nursery ware sets

BEATRIX POTTER
NURSERY AND GIFT WARE SHAPE GUIDE

nless otherwise stated, all the designs are in current production.

URSERY WARE
l introduced in 1987
ee illustration below)

ursery plate 8 inch
bitha Twitchit and Tom Kitten

ursery plate 6 inch
enjamin Bunny in a tam o'shanter
mima Puddle-Duck and
  the Foxy Whiskered Gentleman
bitha Twitchit and Tom Kitten

aby plate
r Jeremy Fisher landing the stickleback

Cereal bowl
Jemima Puddle-Duck
Mr Jeremy Fisher landing the stickleback

Egg cup
Tom Kitten

Nursery tea cup and saucer
Mrs Tittlemouse going to the storeroom
Mrs Tittlemouse looking out of her window

Hug-a-mug with 1 handle
The Flopsy Bunnies

Hug-a-mug with 2 handles
Hunca Munca sweeping

Nursery clock
Tabitha Twitchit and Tom Kitten

ROYAL ALBERT

CHILDREN'S SET

THE WORLD OF BEATRIX POTTER

GIFT BOXED NURSERYWARE SETS

3 Piece Children's Set

2 Piece Baby Set

8in Plate

Baby Plate

2 Handled Hug-a-Mug

Cereal Bowl

1 Handled Hug-a-Mug

NURSERY WARE SETS

Children's set 3 pieces (see illustration above)
Introduced: 1987
Nursery plate 8 inch, cereal bowl and
hug-a-mug with 1 handle

Infant's set 2 pieces (see illustration above)
Introduced: 1987
Baby plate and hug-a-mug with 2 handles

Christening collection
(see illustration below)
Standard designs overprinted with
'Christening Collection'
Introduced: 1991   Withdrawn: 1994
Nursery plate, money ball, baby plate and
hug-a-mug with two handles

CHRISTENING ITEMS

TOM KITTEN

Plate 8"

MR JEREMY FISHER

Baby Plate

Money Ball

Hug-a-Mug
2 Handle

GIFT WARE

Square wall plate 6¼ inch
(see illustrations opposite and below)
Introduced: 1987   Withdrawn: 1993
Benjamin Bunny eating a lettuce leaf
Jemima Puddle-Duck and
    the Foxy Whiskered Gentleman
Mrs Tiggy-Winkle with the birds and animals
Mr Jeremy Fisher eating a butterfly sandwich

Gainsborough plate 8 inch
(see illustrations below and top page 90)
Introduced: 1992
Benjamin Bunny eating a lettuce leaf
Mr Jeremy Fisher landing the stickleback
Jemima Puddle-Duck and
    the Foxy Whiskered Gentleman
Tabitha Twitchit washing Moppet's face

Gainsborough plate 6 inch
(see illustrations below and top page 90)
Introduced: 1989
Benjamin Bunny eating a lettuce leaf
Mr Jeremy Fisher landing the stickleback
Jemima Puddle-Duck and
    the Foxy Whiskered Gentleman
Tabitha Twitchit washing Moppet's face

89

Gainsborough beaker
(see illustration below)
Introduced: 1987
Benjamin Bunny eating a lettuce leaf

Mr Jeremy Fisher landing the stickleback
Jemima Puddle-Duck and
the Foxy Whiskered Gentleman
Tabitha Twitchit washing Miss Moppet's face

Gainsborough tea cup and saucer
(see illustrations above and on page 89)
Introduced: 1987
Benjamin Bunny in a tam o'shanter
Mr Jeremy Fisher arranging his fishing tackle
Tabitha Twitchit and Tom Kitten
Jemima Puddle-Duck

Gainsborough tea pot
(see illustration opposite)
Introduced: 1989
Jemima Puddle-Duck and
    the Foxy Whiskered Gentleman

Gainsborough cream jug
Introduced: 1989
Jemima Puddle-Duck

Gainsborough sugar bowl
Introduced: 1989
Jemima Puddle-Duck
Mr Jeremy Fisher arranging his fishing tackle

Coaster
(see illustration opposite)
Introduced: 1987/1989
Appley Dapply running with pies (1987)
Benjamin Bunny in a tam o'shanter (1989)
Jemima Puddle-Duck (1989)
Mr Jeremy Fisher arranging his fishing tackle
  (1989)

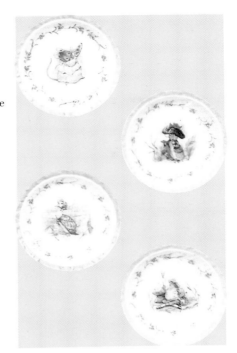

Money ball
(see illustration below)
Introduced: 1987
The Flopsy Bunnies
Hunca Munca sweeping
Jemima Puddle-Duck

Savings book
(see illustration below)
Introduced: 1990
Jemima Puddle-Duck

Peter Rabbit
Watering Can

Mrs Tiggy-Winkle
Kettle

Jemima Puddle-duck
Barrel

Jeremy Fisher
Wheat Vase

Florals
(see illustration above)
Introduced: 1987   Withdrawn: 1992
Barrel with Jemima Puddle-Duck flying
Wheat vase with Mr Jeremy Fisher arranging
his fishing tackle
Watering can with Peter Rabbit eating radishes
Kettle with Mrs Tiggy-Winkle ironing

Keyfobs
(see illustration opposite)
Introduced: 1989   Withdrawn: 1990
Old Mr Brown reading
Mrs Tittlemouse with book
Jemima Puddle-Duck with book
Benjamin Bunny reading
Tom Kitten with book
Mr Jeremy Fisher sitting on a book

GIFT WARE SETS

Afternoon tea set with 3 pieces
Gainsborough plate 6 inch, tea cup and saucer

Tea cup and saucer set with 2 pieces
Gainsborough tea cup and saucer

Teatime set with 3 pieces
Gainsborough tea pot, cream jug and sugar bowl

BEATRIX POTTER
NURSERY AND GIFT WARE SCENES

THE TALE OF PETER RABBIT
1902

Peter eating radishes
Floral

THE TALE OF SQUIRREL NUTKIN
1903

Old Mr Brown reading
Key fob

THE TALE OF BENJAMIN BUNNY
1904

Benjamin Bunny eating a lettuce leaf
Square wall plate 6¼ inch, Gainsborough
plate 8 inch, Gainsborough plate 6 inch,
Gainsborough beaker

Benjamin Bunny in a tam o'shanter
Nursery plate 6 inch, coaster,
Gainsborough tea cup and saucer

Benjamin Bunny reading
Key fob

THE TALE OF TWO BAD MICE
1904

Hunca Munca Sweeping
Hug-a-mug with 2 handles, money ball

THE TALE OF MRS TIGGY-WINKLE
1905

Mrs Tiggy-Winkle with the birds and
animals
Square wall plate 6¼ inch

Mrs Tiggy-Winkle ironing
Floral

THE TALE OF MR JEREMY FISHER
1906

Mr Jeremy Fisher eating a butterfly
sandwich
Square wall plate 6¼ inch

Mr Jeremy Fisher arranging his fishing
tackle
Gainsborough tea cup and saucer, coaster,
sugar bowl, floral

Mr Jeremy Fisher landing the stickleback
Gainsborough plate 8 inch, Gainsborough plate
6 inch, cereal bowl, baby plate, Gainsborough
beaker

Mr Jeremy Fisher sitting on a book
Key fob

THE TALE OF TOM KITTEN
1907

Tabitha Twitchit washing Moppet's face
Gainsborough plate 8 inch, Gainsborough
plate 6 inch, Gainsborough beaker

Tabitha Twitchit and Tom Kitten
Nursery clock, nursery plate 8 inch, nursery
plate 6 inch, Gainsborough tea cup and saucer

Tom Kitten with book
Egg cup, key fob

THE TALE OF JEMIMA PUDDLE-DUCK
1908

Jemima Puddle-Duck
Cereal bowl, coaster, Gainsborough tea cup
and saucer, sugar bowl, cream jug,
money ball, savings book

**Jemima Puddle-Duck and
the Foxy Whiskered Gentleman**
Gainsborough plate 8 inch, Gainsborough
plate 6 inch, square wall plate 6¹/₄ inch,
nursery plate 6 inch, Gainsborough tea pot,
Gainsborough beaker

Jemima Puddle-Duck with book
Key fob

Jemima Puddle-Duck flying
Floral

THE TALE OF THE FLOPSY BUNNIES
1909

The Flopsy Bunnies
Money ball, Hug-a-mug with 1 handle

THE TALE OF MRS TITTLEMOUSE
1910

Mrs Tittlemouse going to the storeroom
Nursery tea cup and saucer

Mrs Tittlemouse looking out of her windo
Nursery tea cup and saucer

Mrs Tittlemouse with a book
Key fob

APPLEY DAPPLY'S NURSERY RHYM
1917

Appley Dapply running with pies
Coaster

*Beatrix Potter's little books
and the figures they inspired*

BEATRIX POTTER'S LITTLE BOOKS AND THE FIGURES THEY INSPIRED

E TALE OF PETER RABBIT 1902
er Rabbit P1098 (1948–C)
s Rabbit P1200 (1951–C)
psy, Mopsy and Cottontail P1274 (1954–C)
er in the Gooseberry Net
57 (1989–1995)
s Rabbit Cooking P3278 (1992–C)
er in Bed P3473 (1995–C)
McGregor P3506 (1995–C)
er Ate a Radish P3533 (1995–C)

E TALE OF SQUIRREL NUTKIN 1903
irrel Nutkin P1102 (1948–C)
Mr Brown P1796 (1963–C)

E TAILOR OF GLOUCESTER 1903
e Tailor of Gloucester P1108 (1949–C)
ly Mouse P1183 (1950–C)
pkin P2508 (1975–1983)
ntleman Mouse Made a Bow
200 (1990–1996)
ly Mouse Made a Curtsy P3220 (1990–C)
More Twist P3325 (1992–C)

E TALE OF BENJAMIN BUNNY 1904
njamin Bunny P1105 (1948–C)
Benjamin Bunny P1940 (1965–C)
Benjamin Bunny and Peter Rabbit P2509
75–1995)
s Rabbit and Bunnies P2543 (1976–C)
orly Peter Rabbit P2560 (1976–C)
njamin Bunny Sat on a Bank
303 (1983–C)
er and the Red Pocket Handkerchief
242 (1991–C)
njamin Ate a Lettuce Leaf P3317 (1992–C)

E TALE OF TWO BAD MICE 1904
nca Munca P1198 (1951–C)

Hunca Munca Sweeping P2584 (1977–C)
Tom Thumb P2989 (1987–C)
Christmas Stocking P3257 (1991–1994)
Hunca Munca Spills the Beads
P3288 (1992–1996)

THE TALE OF MRS TIGGY-WINKLE 1905
Mrs Tiggy-Winkle P1107 (1948–C)
Mrs Tiggy-Winkle Takes Tea P2877 (1985–C)

THE TALE OF THE PIE AND THE PATTY
PAN 1905
Mrs Ribby P1199 (1951–C)
Duchess (with Flowers) P1355 (1955–1967)
Duchess (with Pie) P2601 (1979–1982)
Ribby and the Patty Pan P3280 (1992–C)

THE TALE OF MR JEREMY FISHER 1906
Mr Jeremy Fisher P1157 (1950–C)
Mr Alderman Ptolemy P2424 (1973–C)
Sir Isaac Newton P2425 (1973–1984)
Mr Jeremy Fisher Digging P3090 (1988–1994)

THE STORY OF A FIERCE BAD RABBIT
1906
Fierce Bad Rabbit P2586 (1977–C)

THE STORY OF MISS MOPPET 1906
Miss Moppet P1275 (1954–C)

THE TALE OF TOM KITTEN 1907
Tom Kitten P1100 (1948–C)
Tabitha Twitchit and Miss Moppet
P2544 (1976–1993)
Mr Drake Puddle-Duck P2628 (1979–C)
Mrs Rebecca Puddle-Duck P2647 (1981–C)
Tom Kitten and Butterfly P3030 (1987–1994)
Mittens and Moppet P3197 (1990–1994)

THE TALE OF JEMIMA PUDDLE-DUCK 1908
Jemima Puddle-Duck P1092 (1948–C)
Foxy Whiskered Gentleman P1277 (1954–C)
Jemima Puddle-Duck Made a Feather Nest
P2823 (1983–C)
Jemima Puddle-Duck and Foxy Whiskered
Gentleman P3193 (1990–C)
Foxy Reading Country News P3219 (1990–C)

THE ROLY POLY PUDDING 1908
(Later published as The Tale of Samuel Whiskers
1926)
Samuel Whiskers P1106 (1948–1995)
Tabitha Twitchit P1676 (1961–1995)
Anna Maria P1851 (1963–1983)
Cousin Ribby P2284 (1970–1993)
John Joiner P2965 (1990–C)

THE TALE OF FLOPSY BUNNIES 1909
Mrs Flopsy Bunny P1942 (1965–C)
Thomasina Tittlemouse P2668 (1981–1989)
Benjamin Wakes Up P3234 (1991–C)

THE TALE OF GINGER AND PICKLES 1909
Ginger P2559 (1976–1982)
Pickles P2334 (1971–1982)
Sally Henny Penny P2452 (1974–1993)
Miss Dormouse P3251 (1991–1995)

THE TALE OF MRS TITTLEMOUSE 1910
Mrs Tittlemouse P1103 (1948–1993)
Mr Jackson P2453 (1974–C)
Mother Ladybird P2966 (1989–1996)
Babbitty Bumble P2971 (1989–1993)

THE TALE OF TIMMY TIPTOES 1911
Timmy Tiptoes P1101 (1948–C)
Goody Tiptoes P1675 (1961–C)
Chippy Hackee P2627 (1979–1993)
Goody and Timmy Tiptoes P2957 (1986–1996)

THE TALE OF MR TOD 1912
Tommy Brock P1348 (1955–C)
Old Mr Bouncer P2956 (1986–1995)
Mr Tod P3091 (1988–1993)

THE TALE OF PIGLING BLAND 1913
Pigling Bland P1365 (1955–C)
Aunt Pettitoes P2276 (1970–1993)
Pig Wig P2381 (1972–1982)
Pigling Eats His Porridge P3252 (1991–19?

APPLEY DAPPLY'S NURSERY RHYME 1917
Old Woman Who Lived in a Shoe
P1545 (1959–C)
Amiable Guinea Pig P2061 (1967–1983)
Appley Dapply P2333 (1971–C)
Little Black Rabbit P2585 (1977–C)
Diggory Diggory Delvet P2713 (1982–C)
Old Mr Pricklepin P2767 (1983–1989)
Old Woman Who Lived in a Shoe Knitting
P2804 (1983–C)
Cottontail P2878 (1985–1996)

THE TALE OF JOHNNY TOWN-MOUSE 1918
Timmy Willie P1109 (1949–1993)
Johnny Town-Mouse P1276 (1954–1993)
Timmy Willie Sleeping P2996 (1986–1996)
Johnny Town-Mouse with Bag
P3094 (1988–1994)

CECILY PARSLEY'S NURSERY RHYME 1922
Cecily Parsley P1941 (1965–1993)
And This Pig Had None P3319 (1992–C)

THE TALE OF LITTLE PIG ROBINSON 1930
Little Pig Robinson P1104 (1948–C)
Susan P2716 (1983–1989)
Little Pig Robinson Spying
P3031 (1987–1993)

IN THE MARKET-PLACE
NICK TZIMAS

WHERE TO BUY

Current Royal Albert Beatrix Potter figures are available from specialist china and gift shops in many parts of the world. Royal Albert is part of the Royal Doulton group and details of stockists and other product information can be obtained from one of their Distribution and Sales Companies.

Royal Doulton
Sales Division
Minton House, London Road
Stoke-on Trent ST4 7QD
England

Royal Doulton USA INC.
700 Cottontail Lane
Somerset
NJ 08873, USA

Royal Doulton Canada Ltd
850 Progress Avenue
Scarborough
Ontario M1H 3C4, Canada

Royal Doulton Australia Pty Ltd
17-23 Merriwa Street, Gordon
NSW 2072, Australia

Royal Doulton Europe
Europark Noord 25
B-9100 Sint Niklaas
Belgium

Royal Doulton Dodwell Ltd
No. 35 Kowa Building
14-14 Akasaka
1-Chome, Minato-Ku
Tokyo 107
Japan

Discontinued John Beswick Beatrix Potter figures can be purchased from antique shops, markets and fairs as well as some auction houses. There are specialist dealers in Beswick products who attend the venues and events detailed on the next page but it is also worth browsing at general shops and stalls as well as country auctions.

UK

New Caledonian Market
Bermondsey Square
London SE1
Friday morning
(Nearest tube London Bridge)

Portobello Road Market
London W11
Saturday only
(Nearest tube Notting Hill Gate)

Alfie's Antique Market
13-25 Church Street
London NW8
Tuesday-Saturday
(Nearest tube Edgware Road)

Camden Passage Market
off Upper Street
London N1
Wednesday and Saturday
(Nearest tube Angel)

Louis Taylor Auction House
10 Town Road, Hanley
Stoke-on-Trent

Peter Wilson Auction House
Victoria Gallery
Market Street
Nantwich
Cheshire

**UK Doulton & Beswick
Collectors Fair**
The Queensway Hall, Civic Centre
Dunstable
Bedfordshire
Enquiries: 01394 386663

Stafford International Doulton Fair
Stafford County Showground
Stafford
Enquiries: 0114 2750333

Doulton & Beswick Collectors Fair
The National Motorcycle Museum
Birmingham
Enquiries: 0181 3033316

Alexandra Palace Collectors Fairs
Wood Green
London N22 4AM

USA

Florida Doulton Convention
Fort Lauderdale
Florida
Enquiries: (305) 672 0700

Doulton Show
Holiday Inn
Cherry Hill, New Jersey
Enquiries: (914) 634 8456

Doulton Show
Holiday Inn
Independence
Ohio
Enquiries: (914) 634 8456

Information about general shows and markets can be found in the local press and specialist publications such as *The Antique Trader Weekly*.

CANADA

Harbourfront Antique Market
390 Queens Quay West
Toronto
(Tuesday – Sunday)

Canadian Art and Collectible Show
Kitchener Memorial Auditorium
400 East Avenue, Kitchener
Ontario
Enquiries: 519 364-3217

Information about general fairs and markets can be found in the local press and specialist publications such as *Antique Showcase*.

AUSTRALIA

Various general antique fairs and markets are held throughout the country and information can be found in the local press and specialist publications such as *Carter's Australian Antique Trader*.

PLACES TO VISIT

**Beswick Factory Tour
and Museum**
John Beswick
Gold Street, Longton
Stoke-on-Trent ST3 2JP
For opening times and tour information telephone
(01782) 292292
See also page 101

Beatrix Potter's House
Hill Top
Near Sawrey
Ambleside LA22 0LF
For opening times telephone
Mr Ken Wroe on
(015394) 36269

Beatrix Potter Gallery
Main Street
Hawkshead LA22 0NS
For opening times telephone
(015394) 36355

The World of Beatrix Potter
The Old Laundry
Craig Brow
Bowness-on-Windermere LA23 8BT
For opening times telephone
(015394) 88444

**The House of the Tailor of
Gloucester**
Beatrix Potter Shop and Museum
9 College Court
Gloucester GL1 2NJ
For opening times telephone
(01452) 422856

CLUBS AND SOCIETIES

THE BEATRIX POTTER SOCIETY

This society has a world-wide membership and publishes four newsletters a year which give details of the Society's regular talks and meetings in London, visits to places of interest, reviews of recent books and exhibitions, members' letters and news of Beatrix Potter collections and activities throughout the world.

Membership Secretary
Mrs Margaret Heaton
Heatherdene
30 Alpha Road
Chobham
Woking
Surrey GU24 8NF

USA Liaison Officer
Mrs Jane Morse
7 Webster Road
Orono
Maine 04473

Canadian Liaison Officer
Sheila Campbell
66 Thompson Drive
Box 954 Waterdown
Ontario LOR 2HO

Australian and New Zealand Liaison Officer
Pat Adam
Penguin Books Australia Ltd
487 Maroondah Highway
Ringwood
Victoria 3134

Tree lamp base with Jemima Puddle-Duck figure

Beswick
FACTORY TOURS

ARRANGING YOUR TOUR
To reserve your place you should contact _The Tours Organiser_ (Tel: 01782 291213/292292). Factory tours cost £2.50 per person, and details of reduced rates for groups are available on request.

TOUR TIMES
Tours commence at 10.15am and 2.00pm, Monday to Thursday, and 10.15am and 1.30pm Fridays and are of approximately $1^1/_4$ hours duration. Tours are not available during factory holidays.

For safety reasons, the tour is not available for babies or children under 10 years of age, and children in family groups or school parties must be adequately supervised at all times. Because of the number of stairs the factory is not suitable for elderly or handicapped persons.

MUSEUM
The Beswick Museum is open immediately before tours commence, or by appointment.

SHOP
The Factory Shop is open Monday to Friday, 9.00am to 4.30pm.

Details of tours at other Royal Doulton factories are available on request.

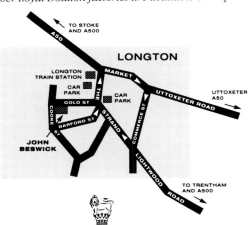

ROYAL DOULTON
John Beswick
• STUDIOS •
Gold Street Longton Stoke-on-Trent ST3 2JP   Telephone: 01782 292292

FURTHER READING

Beswick Collectors Handbook	May, Harvey *(Kevin Francis, 1987)*
The Beswick Price Guide (3rd Edition)	May, Harvey *(Francis Joseph, 1995)*
Royal Doulton Beswick Storybook Figurines (2nd Edition) (Price Guide)	Dale, Jean *(The Charlton Press, 1995)*
Beatrix Potter & Bunnykins Price Guide	Pinchin & Tzimas *(Francis Joseph, 1995)*
Beatrix Potter: Artist, Storyteller and Countrywoman	Taylor, Judy *(Frederick Warne, 1986)*
That Naughty Rabbit	Taylor, Judy *(Frederick Warne, 1987)*
Beatrix Potter's Letters	Taylor, Judy *(Frederick Warne, 1989)*
Letters to Children from Beatrix Potter	Taylor, Judy *(Frederick Warne, 1992)*
Beatrix Potter 1866-1943 The Artist and Her World	Taylor, Whalley, Hobbs & Battrick *(Frederick Warne, 1987)*
Beatrix Potter — The V&A Collection	Hobbs & Whalley *(The Victoria and Albert Museum and Frederick Warne, 1985)*
A Victorian Naturalist: Beatrix Potter's Watercolour Drawings from the Armitt Collection	Jay, Hobbs & Noble *(Frederick Warne, 1992)*
The Magic Years of Beatrix Potter	Lane, Margaret *(Frederick Warne, 1978)*

All Beatrix Potter's Little Books are currently in print with Frederick Warne

COLOUR SECTION INDEX

COLLECTORS NOTES